THE UNHOLY TRINITY UNMASKED

THE UNHOLY TRINITY UNMASKED

Stephen Q. Anthony

Published by Know the Truth Media
knowthetruthmedia@gmail.com

ISBN: 978-0-578-37616-5

Unless otherwise noted, all Scripture quotations are from the King James Bible.

Table of Contents

Prologue

Invasion from Outer Space!

This thought has captured the imaginations of people even before this current generation of 'Star Trekkies', Star Wars fans, and NASA Scientists searching for intelligent life on other planets. One bumper sticker posed the question 'Is there any intelligent life on this planet?'

On October 30, 1938 Orson Welles narrated an episode of The War of the Worlds, a book written by H.G. Wells. It was performed as a Halloween special on Mercury Theatre on the Air. It was done so realistically, that many in the radio audience thought it was a news report and hysteria ensued. While this was simply science fiction, many today in the highest levels of government are seriously considering that alien life may exist in the far reaches of the galaxy. In 2020 President Donald J. Trump initiated a new branch of the military; the Space Force. While primarily designed to protect our satellite assets from foreign governments, many in NASA are also concerned about extraterrestrials. They wonder if alleged aliens would be friend or foe and what future interaction might entail.

Years ago, in studying the Bible I came to a startling discovery: We have already been invaded by aliens from outer space! The fact that so few people realize it is a great credit to the aliens' awesome power of stealth and deception. The record shows that in millennia past, Planet Earth was invaded and infiltrated by a vast army from the far reaches of the universe. They are far superior to human beings in both power and

1

intelligence and they number in excess of 50 million. You may at this point think that I am joking or mad, but I assure you that I am neither. This vast alien armada is invisible, operating in dimensions which we are mostly unfamiliar with. Worst of all, however, is that their ultimate goal is the total destruction of the human race. Where did they come from and what is their source of power? Why hasn't the government or the news media informed us of them? Do these aliens have any vulnerability, and if so, what? What are the odds of defeating them? If they are real, why don't more people know about them?

In our lifetime we are seeing their plan come to the forefront with the rise of an Unholy Trinity, comprised of their leader, in collaboration with two human beings. Their leader is known as Satan, who commands a vast army of aliens we know as devils. He will counterfeit the true Trinity with an Antichrist and False Prophet, completing his trio. They are soon to be revealed, heading up a dictatorial one world government and church (New World Order-NWO). There is hope for those who know of their plan and take action to thwart it, but certain destruction for everyone else.

Can there be any truth to all this? Many thousands down through the years would respond with a loud yes! Absolutely! The multitudes that possess this knowledge have included some of the greatest scientific minds, politicians, and scholars of history. You may choose to read no further and say this is all a fairy tale, but I propose to you, what if it is not? What if there is a powerful alien being, (Devil) working in conjunction with human agencies and individuals? Could this be the explanation for the suffering, wars, and problems plaguing the human race? Could this relate to matters as serious as our high crime rate, the many pandemics, wars, and poverty? Could this have anything to do with problems in our educational system, our often-unjust justice system, a political system with opposite platforms but similar results? Could it have anything to do with Communism, Socialism, Nazism, and Humanism? How about the economic crisis, terrorism crisis, or health care crisis? How about the elitist news media constantly pushing false narratives or an entertainment media with no real restraints on their honesty and morality? Is the dramatic rise of witchcraft, Satanism, and the occult a figment of our imagination? The time has come to expose the Unholy Trinity for those who desire to know the truth, and repel Invasion Earth!

Introduction
The Trinity

The concept and reality of the trinity is a fascinating one. The Bible shows us that God is a trinity and man is a trinity created in his image. To a great degree, much of creation is based upon this trinity model. The first verse of the Bible, Genesis 1:1, tells us, *In the beginning, God created the heaven and the earth.* In Genesis 1:26, *And God said Let us make man in our image, after our likeness*: Man was created a trinity, after the image and likeness of God. We were created with a soul(will), a body(flesh), and a spirit. We are three in one. Have you ever talked to yourself? (It is okay to talk to yourself and even answer yourself, but if you catch yourself saying huh, then you're in trouble.) God exists as God the Father, (the head or will), God the Son, (Jesus-God manifested in the flesh), and the Holy Spirit. 1 John 5:7 states, *For there are three that bear record in heaven, the Father, the Word (Jesus), and the Holy Ghost: and these three are one.* (By the way, this verse has been removed from most of the modern Bible versions). The first chapter of the Gospel of John reveals that the *Word* is the Lord Jesus Christ. We are three distinct entities and yet only one person, even as God is.

The universe was created based on this trinity model. For instance:

The universe is composed of space, matter, and time.

Space is composed of solar systems, each of which consists of a sun, planets, and moons.

Matter exists in 3 states: solid, liquid, and gas, and is measured in height, width, and depth (3 dimensional). The building block of matter, the atom, is composed of protons, neutrons, and electrons. Our earth is composed of land, water, and air.

Time consists of past, present, and future. A day consists of seconds, minutes, and hours, while a year consists of days, weeks, and months.

Human beings are a trinity both spiritually and physically. While we are a soul, body, and spirit, physically our body is composed of a head, torso (body), and extremities, (arms & legs). Is this true of the animal kingdom? (Head, body, legs)? Are birds composed of head, body, and extremities (wings & legs)? Fish? (Head, body, fins and tail)? Insects? (Head, body, legs)? Plants? (Roots, trunk, and leaves/fruit/flowers)? Is this a coincidence or the design of a supreme creator?

Satan, the enemy of God, will raise up a counterfeit trinity in opposition to God. It is composed of Satan, (the god of this world), the Antichrist, also called the Beast, and the False Prophet. A fallen angel and 2 mortal men will stand against the almighty God. This unholy trinity is likely in operation now, though not yet revealed. Each of the 3 personages makes a very intriguing study as individuals, and we will begin with their head, Satan.

Part One

The Devil – Satan

Chapter 1

The Devil's Design

Devil- take off the D and you have evil! What is evil? If there is a Devil, where did he come from? Why would God create an enemy, let alone one so evil? What are his powers and limitations? Is he able to defeat God? What does he have to do with me anyway; I live in a physical world? These are questions that occurred to me when I began to face the fact that there was a spiritual dimension about which I knew very little. I could pretend it was all science fiction, but careful scientific reasoning seemed to make the Bible account very logical, if not downright obvious.

God never created Satan, the Devil. He created a multitude of incredible beings known as angels, to be ministering spirits. They are often misnamed as aliens and ghosts. One of these angels excelled all others in beauty, power, and position. His name was Lucifer. Here is what the Bible says about his design:

> *Moreover, the word of the LORD came unto me, saying, Son of man, take up a lamentation upon the king of Tyrus, and say unto him, Thus saith the Lord GOD; Thou sealest up the sum, full of wisdom, and perfect in*

beauty. Thou hast been in Eden the garden of God; every precious stone was thy covering, the sardius, topaz, and the diamond, the beryl, the onyx, and the jasper, the sapphire, the emerald, and the carbuncle, and gold: the workmanship of thy tabrets and of thy pipes was prepared in thee in the day that thou wast created. Thou art the anointed cherub that covereth and I have set thee so: thou wast upon the holy mountain of God; thou hast walked up and down in the midst of the stones of fire. Thou wast perfect in thy ways from the day that thou wast created till iniquity was found in thee. (Ezekiel 28:11-15)

God addresses Lucifer here as the king of Tyrus. He is doing this symbolically or the king of Tyrus may have been possessed by Satan. In either case it is obvious that God is not speaking of a mortal man. No man is covered with every precious stone and has built in tabrets and pipes, which are musical instruments. Also, he was *the anointed cherub*, and was in the holy mountain of God. A *cherub* is an angel of the order of cherubim. A study of Isaiah 14 reveals that both passages are talking about the same creature. Lucifer had the exalted position of the *anointed cherub that covereth*, the number one angel in heaven. In other words, he was God's honor guard and song leader, leading all angels in praise and worship of Almighty God. To this end, he was equipped with built in *tabrets*, (tambourine type instruments), and *pipes*, most likely producing sounds far surpassing the most sophisticated pipe organ or synthesizer on earth. He was the most beautiful and perfectly created being in the universe, surpassing all others in beauty, position, power, and wisdom. For all this, he was still a creature, created by God.

God's creation was all very good. God is not to blame for the sin, misery and the problems of mankind any more than General Motors is to blame for a wrecked Cadillac. Satan has been very successful at casting aspersions at God, but he is the bad guy, not God!

Though God created Lucifer perfect in beauty, and full of wisdom, he also created him with a free will. God never desired to create robotic angels or humans, but creatures that would love and serve him of their own volition. The incredible power and abilities God invested in Lucifer could be used for good or evil. Ultimately through pride, he chose to usurp God's authority, rebelling against him and using his powers for evil. Among his many powers are the ability to persuade, deceive, and destroy.

Consider his powers of persuasion. He was able to persuade 1/3 of the highly intelligent angelic host to rebel against their Creator and follow himself. We find this in Revelation 12:3-4,7,9

> V3 *And there appeared another wonder in heaven; and behold a great red dragon, having seven heads and ten horns, and seven crowns upon his heads. V4 And his tail drew the third part of the stars (angels) of heaven, and did cast them to the earth: and the dragon stood before the woman which was ready to be delivered, for to devour her child as soon as it was born. V7 And there was war in heaven: Michael and his angels fought against the dragon; and the dragon fought and his angels, V9 And the great dragon was cast out, that old serpent, called the Devil, and Satan, which deceiveth the whole world: he was cast out into the earth, and his angels were cast out with him.*

Notice they were no longer God's angels, but Satan's angels, (devils). To pull off such a feat, he was obviously the epitome of the super salesman, with incredible powers of persuasion. How could anyone persuade an intelligent being to rebel against an almighty and all loving God? It should not be too hard to imagine since so many are doing it today with such ease. Lucifer could have sold ice cubes to Eskimos in Alaska.

Not the least of his powers, are his powers of deception. After all, he deceived Eve in the garden of Eden with the lie that if she disobeyed God and ate of the forbidden fruit, not only would she not die, but she and Adam could become as gods.

More dangerous are his powers of destruction. In John 10:10, Jesus said of him, *The thief cometh not, but for to steal, and to kill, and to destroy*: A small glimpse of this is shown in the book of Job (Jobe), where Satan asked permission of God to make miserable the life of this man named Job. In this story he brought fire from heaven, bands of marauders, and a tornado, to destroy Job's children, servants, and material wealth. He has the power to destroy all of mankind in short order, but fortunately his great power is limited by God's permission.

You may ask how such a perfect being, with such an exalted position, could rebel and lose it all? How did Lucifer, the *anointed cherub*, become Satan, the adversary of God? Let's consider the Devil's downfall.

Chapter 2

The Devil's Downfall

Pride and the 5 I Will's

G od created angels and man with their own free will; with the privilege and power to choose. At some point Lucifer's beauty, power, and position went to his head, and he desired God's position and worship. He chose to exalt himself with five statements of the will:

> *How art thou fallen from heaven, O Lucifer, son of the morning! how art thou cut down to the ground, which didst weaken the nations! For thou hast said in thine heart, I will ascend into heaven, I will exalt my throne above the stars of God: I will sit also upon the mount of the congregation, in the sides of the north: I will ascend above the heights of the clouds; I will be like the most High. Yet thou shalt be brought down to hell, to the sides of the pit.* (Isaiah 14:12-15)

Satan's downfall was in attempting to usurp God's position through pride. We do the same by relegating God to an inferior position in our lives. Fortunately, God's position was not available, and Lucifer lost his own position as the anointed cherub. Unfortunately, he didn't lose his power, intellect, or access to God. He persuaded one third of the angels of heaven to follow him and today we know these fallen angels as devils, with their leader, Satan, being referred to as the Devil. *And his tail drew the third part of the stars* (angels*) of heaven, and did cast them to the earth* (Revelation 12:4): God could have immediately judged these devils and cast them into the hell he created for them. In his matchless wisdom, he instead chose to allow their challenge to his authority to be played out completely. In this way, God has allowed everyone to choose sides so that all of creation will witness the vast difference between God's way and Satan's way. We learn in Proverbs 16:25, *There is a way that seemeth right unto a man, but the end thereof are the ways of death.*

As the most beautiful, powerful, intelligent being ever created, the Devil controls a vast army. By studying Revelation 5:11, *And I beheld, and I heard the voice of many angels round about the throne and the beasts and the elders: and the number of them was ten thousand times ten thousand, and thousands of thousands*; and doing some simple math, we find the remaining number of angels worshiping God is ten thousand times ten thousand or over one hundred million, plus *thousands of thousands*. Hence, we conclude that one third of the angels (stars) who fell was at least fifty million. Wow, what a formidable army. No mortal man is able to stand against them in his own power. There is a name, however, which causes Satan and his host to tremble, the name of Jesus.

The Bible teaches: *That at the name of Jesus every knee should bow, of things in heaven, and things in earth, and things under the earth; And that every tongue should confess that Jesus Christ is Lord, to the glory of God the Father* (Philippians 2:10,11).

Why is this name used as a curse word, if Jesus was just a teacher or prophet? Why not use Confucius, Buddha, Mohammed, or Hitler as curse words? Did you ever hear someone

14

exclaim, Buddha, or oh Hitler, when they were frustrated? The fact is that Jesus is the Creator and all-powerful God, and Satan hates him and his name. Therefore, people under Satan's influence naturally follow his lead.

How unfortunate that Satan's downfall led to man's downfall. Adam and Eve, who were the first man and woman created by God had one simple rule to obey in the garden of Eden. This was to trust him and not eat from the fruit of only one tree, the *Tree of the Knowledge of Good and Evil*. God even showed Adam a re-creation so he knew who God was and that He was the Creator. This passage has been used by skeptics to try to prove the Bible inaccurate and cast doubt. Let's examine this apparent contradiction and God's re-creation or second creation:

In Genesis, Chapter 1, verses 11-13, God created trees on day 3. In verses 20-23, the Bible says God created the fowls (birds) on day 5. In verses 24-26 and verse 31, the Bible says God created the animals and then man on day 6.

However, in Chapter 2, verses 7-9, the Bible says God created the trees after man. In verses 18-22, the Bible says that God created every beast (animal) and fowl (bird) out of the ground and brought them to Adam to name. Therefore, these animals and birds were created after Adam, and after that God created Eve. This certainly seems to be a contradiction compared to chapter one! There are no contradictions in the Bible, only apparent contradictions. The explanation is really quite simple and lies in Chapter 2, verse 8. After His initial creation, God planted a garden in Eden and put Adam in it. He then re-created one of each tree, animal and bird and had Adam name each one. For instance, dog, cat, giraffe, bear, eagle, dove, etc. The last one to be created was Eve, literally taken from Adam's side, through the first anesthesia and surgery. Why did God perform this second creation? Since Adam was created last during the initial 6 days of creation, he would not be sure that God created everything. Satan could have come along and claimed to be the creator and Adam would not be sure. God planted a garden and put Adam in it and showed him how he created the trees, animals and birds, so Adam would be sure who the Creator was. Eve was taken from Adam after this and so did not see God create anything. Adam may not have properly communicated this to his wife, (things haven't changed, have they ladies?), and so it is no surprise that Satan approached Eve with his deception, not Adam. Satan persuaded Eve and Eve persuaded Adam. Someone said man is the head, but woman is the neck that makes the head turn. Someone else wisely said that the stronger sex is actually the weaker sex, because the weakness of the stronger sex is the weaker sex. Doubletalk with truth.

Satan is a master of persuasion and Adam and Eve were no match. Their only hope was to believe, trust, and obey God. They blew it and ate the only fruit in the garden which God had forbidden, the fruit from the *Tree of the Knowledge of Good and Evil*. (By the way; it wasn't an apple). Satan had cast doubt on God's Word and convinced Eve that God was withholding His best and she could be a god. In their fall, Satan gained the dominion of planet Earth. Before this Adam and Eve had dominion (ownership) over the whole earth, not just a plot of real estate on the French Riviera or the island of Manhattan, or the gold coast of Florida or California. Also consider the mineral wealth they owned like gold, silver, diamonds, and other precious gems. They lost it all, along with their purity, innocence, eternal life, and most importantly, their relationship with God.

Satan won a major victory when sin came into the world. Prior to this Adam had all the advantages and lost them all with one bite. Now Satan's desire becomes evident as Jesus warned in John 10:10 *The thief (Devil) cometh not, but for to steal, and to kill, and to destroy.* Satan now took dominion and owned the keys of death and hell. Adam was created to live forever, but now he was dead spiritually and began the long and gruesome process of dying physically. Now all the advantages go to Satan as he becomes the *god of this world* (2Corinthians 4:4). What would he now do? What would be his desire as the

16

new ruler of planet Earth?

Chapter 3

The Devil's Desire

The devil hates God, and desires His exalted position, but what can the Devil do? The position is not available and who can do anything to God? I heard a riddle: What is greater than God; more evil than the Devil; rich people need it; poor people have it; and if you eat it you will die! What is it? The answer is NOTHING! That is also what Satan can do directly to God. Since Satan can't hurt God, he focuses his attention and hatred on us who are created in God's image, his crown of creation. The devil's desire was best described by Jesus in John 10:10, when he said, *the thief cometh not, but for to steal, and to kill, and to destroy:* What are some evidences of this? There are many: from the drunk who kills an innocent family with his automobile, to the teenage girl who loses her purity and becomes pregnant out of marriage, to the super rich elitist who performs human sacrifice in a Satanic ritual. Space would not permit me to share all the examples of each of us who have been deceived and ripped off by Satan in his effort to *steal, kill, and destroy.* Satan delights in stealing from people. Teenage pregnancy is epidemic in our society with the regrettable result of over 1 ½ million babies being slaughtered through abortion each year. Marriages often have little chance of success, with children being the innocent victims in a divorce. Broken hearts and despair abound because so many are ignorant of God's wonderful plan and provision.

Think of the many who spend hard earned money gambling it away in casinos or on lottery tickets, hoping to get rich quick. A recent bumper sticker I saw said that the Lottery was a tax for those who never learned math. How sad, but true. Satan uses the lure of hitting it big to steal billions from those who cannot afford it. Consider the billions who are in bondage to pornography, alcohol, drugs, power, position, fame, and false religion to name a few. Instead of investing in God's eternity and special plan for their life, they squander their time and life on the temporary peanuts which Satan tosses out to them. Satan's desire is to steal us blind, whether it is time, money, or virtue and destroy us at his first opportunity. He has a great many weapons he uses to accomplish his nefarious desire and one of the most effective is his deceptions.

Chapter 4

The Devil's Deceptions

In Satan's desire to hurt and destroy God's human creation, he employs various weapons. Though many of these are incredibly powerful, such as the forces of nature, none compare to his greatest weapon, which is deception. His main target is the heart or mind of man, and nothing is so effective in corrupting it as deceit. The Bible tells us in John 8:44, *he is a liar, and the father of it.* His first attack upon mankind was through deception in the garden of Eden when he approached Eve in the form of a serpent. (At that time there was no fear between man and animals.) Satan first cast doubt on, and confused God's Word, when he said, *Yea, hath God said, Ye shall not eat of every tree of the garden* (Genesis 3:1)? That was not what God had said. When Eve corrected him, he secondly disputed what God said. He lied and said, *Ye shall not surely die* (Genesis 3:4). Then thirdly, he added another deception, with a seductive lie. He said, *For God doth know that in the day ye eat thereof, then your eyes shall be opened, and ye shall be as gods, knowing good and evil* (Genesis 3:5). In this he was accusing God of holding out on them, and tempted her with the fear of loss. It has been said that the fear of loss is a more powerful motivator oftentimes than the desire for gain. This is a common sales technique (we will be out of stock on the sale item by tomorrow), and it worked on Eve. When Eve believed the Devil instead of God and ate the forbidden fruit and shared it with her husband, they both realized too late that they had been deceived. The results of this small deception were enormous. First, they died spiritually, losing their relationship with

God. Second, they lost their immortal life and began the process of dying. Third, they brought sin and death into the human race, and a curse upon our planet, with the resultant suffering. God explains it like this in Romans 5:12, *Wherefore, as by one man sin entered into the world, and death by sin; and so death passed upon all men, for that all have sinned.* Every person ever born of a human father has been born with a sin nature due to Adam's transgression. Jesus is the only exception as he was supernaturally conceived through a virgin.

Satan uses the same techniques today of casting doubt on God's Word, the Bible; of confusing what the Bible says; and making people believe that if they listen to God from the Bible, they will be missing out on all that life has to offer. I remember an old beer commercial that said, You only go around once, so grab all the gusto you can get, implying that you would miss out on some wonderful fun in life if you didn't drink their beer. Like many of Satan's lies, reality is usually the opposite.

Let's examine just a few of Satan's most popular deceptions that he is using today, and you will see how they are the same deceptions he used on Eve in the Garden of Eden.

HUMANISM

In a nutshell, Humanism is a philosophy that asserts the greatness of man and discounts God. It is best illustrated by a statement in the Humanist Manifesto, which states in part, "No God will save us. We must save ourselves." We can see in this statement how Satan disputes God's claim that man is a sinner in need of a Savior. Romans 5:8 states, *But God commendeth his love toward us, in that, while we were yet sinners, Christ died for us.*

Dr. Tim LaHaye, well known preacher and co-author of the Left Behind series, wrote an excellent book in 1980 entitled the Battle for the Mind, in which he thoroughly explains and exposes Satan's deception of humanism. It should be required reading for all school teachers.

One of our country's most famous humanists was John

Dewey. He is known as the Father of Progressive Education and was the first president of the American Humanist Association. He also was a declared atheist, who believed that truth is relative. He signed the Humanist Manifesto in 1933 and laid the groundwork for changing our school system from a Biblical foundation to Progressive Education and Humanism.

The Devil's use of Humanism becomes clearer as we examine a magazine article 50 years later showing the true aims of this dangerous philosophy:

"The battle for humankind's future must be waged and won in the public-school classroom by teachers who correctly perceive their role as the proselytizers of a new faith: a religion of humanity that recognizes and respects the spark of what theologians call divinity in every human being. These teachers must embody the same selfless dedication as the most rabid fundamentalist preachers, for they will be ministers of another sort, utilizing a classroom instead of a pulpit to convey humanist values in whatever subject they teach, ... The classroom must and will become an arena of conflict between the old and the new -the rotting corpse of Christianity, together with all its adjacent evils and misery, and the new faith of humanism, resplendent in its promise of a world in which the never-realized Christian ideal of "love thy neighbor" will finally be achieved."[1]

Initially, our schools had a Biblical foundation for education. For example, ten of the twelve presidents of Harvard, prior to the Revolutionary War, were ministers[2], and according to reliable calculations, over fifty percent of the seventeenth-century Harvard graduates became ministers.[3] Of note is the fact that 106 of the first 108 schools in America were founded on the Christian faith.[4]

In the mid 1960's, however, this Christian foundation was

replaced by Humanism as the Bible, Prayer, and later the Ten Commandments were expelled from our public school system. Let's look for a minute at the results of this paradigm shift in the public schools.

A study was done revealing the top offenses of public-school students in 1940, prior to the shift to Humanism.[5] The offenses were as follows:

(1) Talking
(2) Chewing gum
(3) Running in the halls
(4) Wearing improper clothing
(5) Making noise
(6) Not putting paper in wastebaskets
(7) Getting out of turn in line

Compare that list to the top offenses of students forty years later, in 1980:

(1) Rape
(2) Robbery
(3) Assault
(4) Personal theft
(5) Burglary
(6) Drug abuse
(7) Arson
(8) Bombings
(9) Alcohol abuse
(10) Carrying of weapons
(11) Absenteeism
(12) Vandalism
(13) Murder
(14) Extortion
(15) Gang warfare
(16) Pregnancies
(17) Abortions
(18) Suicide

(19) Venereal disease
(20) Lying and cheating

    Having been in school in the 50's and 60's, I saw firsthand the reality of this change, as most folks 60 or older can attest. Today, middle schools and high schools have police officers on duty in each school. That was unnecessary before the mid 60's.

    How have social issues been influenced by humanism in our society? Notice the difference since our Christian foundation was officially abandoned in the schools in 1963-64.

Unmarried Couples
Up 536%

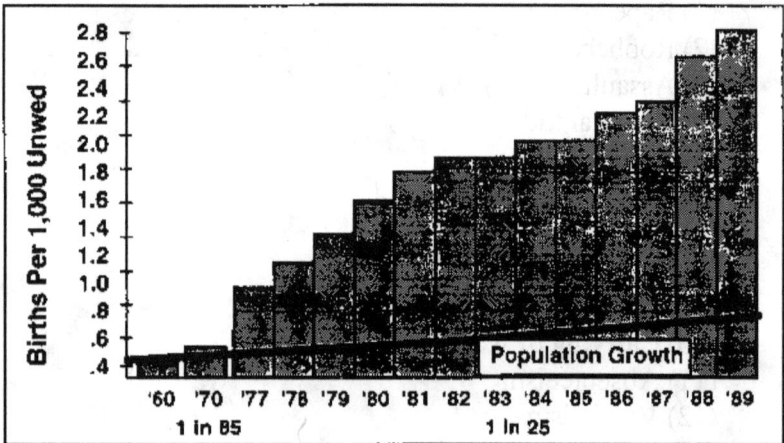

Divorce Rates

Up 117%

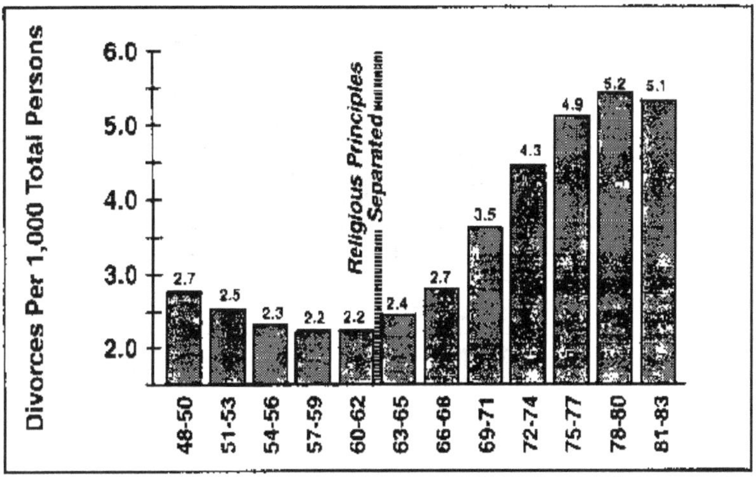
Divorces Per 1,000 Total Persons
6.0
5.0
4.0
3.0
2.0
2.7
2.5
2.3
2.2
2.2
2.4
2.7
3.5
4.3
4.9
5.2
5.1
Religious Principles Separated
48-50
51-53
54-56
57-59
60-62
63-65
66-68
69-71
72-74
75-77
78-80
81-83

Unwed Birth Rates

Pregnancies to Girls 10-14 Up 553%

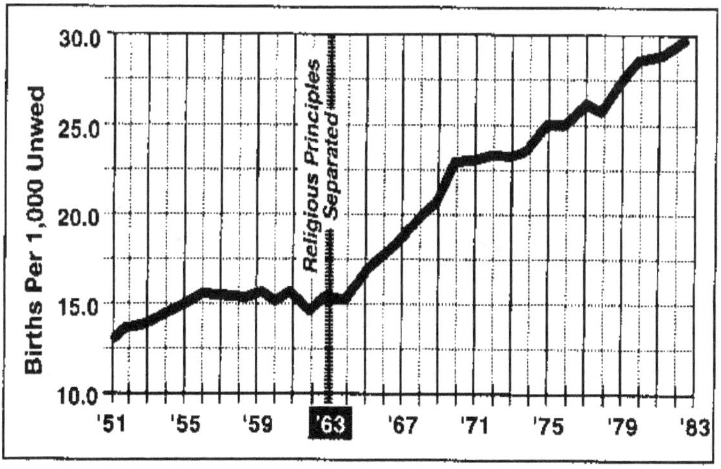
Births Per 1,000 Unwed
30.0
25.0
20.0
15.0
10.0
Religious Principles Separated
'51
'55
'59
'63
'67
'71
'75
'79
'83

Sexually Transmitted Diseases
Gonorrhea: Ages 15-19, Up 226%

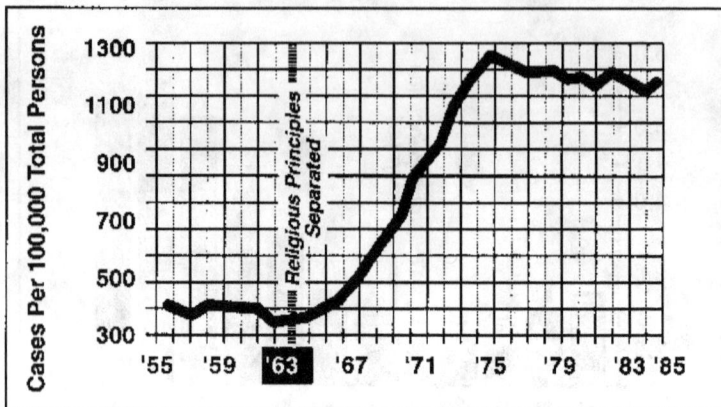

Cases Per 100,000 Total Persons

1300
1100
900
700
500
300

'55 '59 63 '67 '71 '75 '79 '83 '85

Religious Principles Separated

Violent Crime Offenses
Up 794%

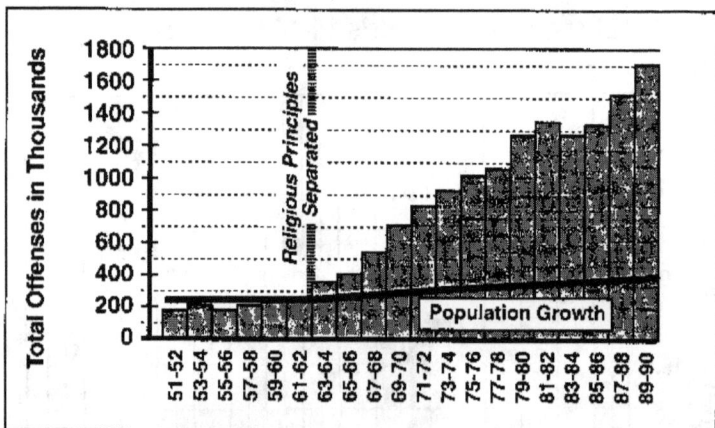

Total Offenses in Thousands

1800
1600
1400
1200
1000
800
600
400
200
0

51-52 53-54 55-56 57-58 59-60 61-62 63-64 65-66 67-68 69-70 71-72 73-74 75-76 77-78 79-80 81-82 83-84 85-86 87-88 89-90

Religious Principles Separated

Population Growth

28

Scholastic Aptitude Test Scores
Decline in Student Achievement

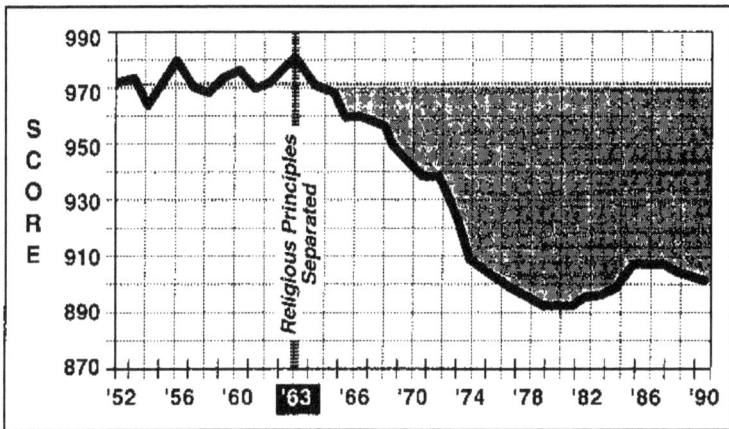

Since the year 2000, there have been over 150 school shootings resulting in hundreds of deaths. Are the causes guns or may it be the absence of Biblical teaching, replaced with the teachings of godless humanism, and evolution, combined with the violence promoted in music, tv, movies, and video games?

Let's revisit the statement in the Humanist Magazine: "the rotting corpse of Christianity, together with all its adjacent evils and misery, and the new faith of humanism, resplendent in its promise of a world in which the never-realized Christian ideal of love thy neighbor will finally be achieved". Should the extreme hypocrisy of their statement be a surprise? This is strikingly reminiscent of Satan's lie to Eve that in disobeying God she would not die, but instead become *as gods*. The truth is that all of the suffering and misery of mankind emanate from Eve believing the lie of Satan instead of God. God accurately identifies Satan's character in John 8:44, *He was a murderer from the beginning, and abode not in the truth, because there is no truth in him.* Humanism is certainly a deadly deception that Satan is using to turn people from the God who loves and cares for them.

Evolution

Unfortunately, Humanism is only one of Satan's multi-faceted attacks through deception. A close cousin is the theory of Evolution. Evolution simply stated is the belief that our complex universe, from the vast expanse of galactic star systems to the intricate sub-microscopic world is the result of accidental processes over billions of years with no intelligent design and purpose behind them. The greatest enemy to evolution is not the Bible but rather common sense. If it were not for indoctrination from preschool through post graduate studies, it is doubtful to me that any thinking person would believe it. When I look into the night sky and observe the Big and Little Dippers, it seems rather obvious that the alignment of these stars is the result of some intelligent design. The Bible states in Psalm 19:1, *The heavens declare the glory of God; and the firmament sheweth his handywork.* In other words, common sense in observing nature and its wonders shows that there is an incredible Creator, behind the order, precision and beauty in our universe and world.

When someone looks at an I-phone or a Rolls Royce automobile, they know that there were some skilled craftsmen and engineers involved in their creation. The human body alone is infinitely more complex than these. Sir Isaac Newton used the eye as an illustration. It is the only transparent member in the body. On the outside it has a hard transparent skin and within, transparent humors, with a crystalline lens in the middle and a pupil before the lens, all of them so finely shaped and fitted for vision that the study of it has enabled man to invent the modern camera. Did blind chance know that there was light and what was its refraction, and fit the eyes of all creatures to take advantage of it? Common sense screams NO! This is only one simple example of thousands which could be given. Examine any of the systems of the human body: circulatory, respiratory, digestive, etc. You will find they are incredibly complex systems involving amazing chemical and electrical processes. Newton's Second Law of Thermodynamics is commonly known as the Law of Increased Entropy. It states that matter and energy deteriorate over time. In other words, all matter tends towards a state of disorder. This is easily observable in our world. Leave your lawn alone for a year and does it evolve to be more beautiful or deteriorate? How about your automobile or home? The answer is obvious. They all require constant maintenance. The theory of evolution is contradicted by this one law alone.

While common sense and Newton's law dispute evolution, let's examine some additional scientific evidence concerning the age of the earth. Evolutionary theory suggests that the universe is billions of years old and resulted from a cosmic explosion where all the matter of the universe was condensed to the size of a period on this page (according to Elementary School science textbooks). The enormously compact dot of matter started to spin, then exploded, resulting in the incredibly beautiful constellations, stars and planets all traveling in precise orbits.

Because this deception has become a cornerstone of our public education system, we should examine it closely. Dr. Kent Hovind of Creation Science Evangelism has done a great job providing logical and scientific information refuting the theory of evolution. The following information is taken with his permission, from his Creation Seminar Notebook:

Universe Not "Billions of Years Old"

Facts/Proof from Science

The general theory of evolution is based on several faulty assumptions. (Note: It is important to understand by this statement that we are not disputing simple variations that some call "microevolution," whose micro-changes are often observed but never lead to a fundamentally different kind of plant or animal.)

Easy to prove wrong among the assumptions of the theory of evolution are the following:

- that the universe is billions of years old,
- that life comes from nonliving minerals,
- that mutations create or improve a species,
- that natural selection has creative power.

In this section we will deal with the first of these assumptions. The others will be dealt with elsewhere. If, in fact, it could be demonstrated that the universe is not billions of years old, all other arguments about evolution become meaningless and unnecessary.

In children's fairy tales, we are told FROG + MAGIC SPELL (usually a kiss) = PRINCE.

In modern science (?) textbooks we are told that FROG + TIME = PRINCE. The same basic fairy tale is being promoted in textbooks today, but the new magic potion cited is TIME. When the theory of evolution is discussed, TIME is the panacea for all the thousands of problems that arise.

In nearly all discussions and debates about evolution that I (Dr. Kent Hovind) have held at universities and colleges, I ask the evolutionists how certain things could have evolved by chance. Their answer is nearly always, "Given enough time ...." TIME is the evolutionists' god. TIME is able to accomplish anything the evolutionists can dream up. TIME can easily turn a frog into a prince. TIME can create matter from nothing and life from matter. TIME can create order from chaos (at least they believe it can).

But let's remove TIME from the above equation. There are three results:

Evolution becomes impossible obviously (even if the universe were billions of years old, evolution remains impossible).

Evolutionists will holler like a baby whose pacifier has been pulled out because they know that if time is removed, their religion (evolution is a religion, not part of science) is silly.

Creation becomes the only reasonable explanation for the existence of this complex universe.

Just One Proof of a Young Earth Settles the Case Against Evolution

Let's imagine we are exploring an old gold mine and we find a Casio Databank watch half buried in the mud on the floor of the mine. Suppose also that the correct time and date are displayed on the watch and it is still running smoothly. Then imagine that I tell you the watch has been there for over one thousand years.

"That's impossible!" you say. "That watch could not have been there for a thousand years and I can prove it!"

"How can you prove I'm wrong?" I say.

"Well, for one thing, this mine was just dug 150 years ago," you say.

"Okay," I admit, "you're right about the thousand years being too much, but the watch has been here for 150 years at least!"

"No!" you say. "Casio didn't make the Databank watch until twelve years ago."

"All right," I say. "The watch was dropped here twelve years ago then." "Impossible!" you say. "The batteries only last five years on that watch, and it's still running. That proves it has been here less than five years."

While we still can't prove exactly when the watch was left there, you have logically limited the date the watch was left to within the last five years. The larger numbers prove nothing in this debate. Even if I were to carbon-date the mud or the plastic in the watch to try to prove that it was thousands of years old, my data would be meaningless. The same logic can be applied to finding the age of the earth. If several factors (actually only one) limit the age of the earth to a few thousand years, the earth cannot be older than that! Even if a few indicators seem to show a greater age for the earth, it only takes ONE proof of a young earth to prove the earth is young.

The Bible teaching is as follows: God created the universe about 6000 years ago.

This creation was ex nihilo (out of nothing) in six literal, twenty-four-hour days. Then, about 4400 years ago, the earth was destroyed by a worldwide Flood. This devastating, year-long flood was responsible for the sediment layers being deposited (the water was going and returning, Gen. 8:3-5). As the mountains rose and the oceans sank in after the Flood (Psalm 104:5-8, Gen. 8:1), the waters rushed off the rising mountains into the new ocean basins. This rapid-erosion topography we still see today, in places like the Grand Canyon. The uniformitarian assumption that today's slow erosion rates that take place through solid rock are the same as has always been, is faulty logic, and ignores catastrophes like the Flood. (2 Peter 3:3-8 says the scoffers are "willingly ignorant" of the Flood.)

Listed below are some of the factors from various branches of science that limit the age of the universe (and the earth) to within the last few thousand years. Though it cannot be scientifically proven exactly when the universe was created, its age can be limited easily to within a few thousand years. Each of the following evidences of a young earth is described in great detail in the books referred to at the end of this section. (Anyone wanting more information should consult these sources at the end.) Source number and page number are given for the following statements. Sources are listed at end.

Evidence From Space

The shrinking sun limits the earth-sun relationship to less than "millions of years." The sun is losing both mass and diameter. Changing the mass would upset the fine gravitational balance that keeps the earth just the right distance for life to survive.[6] (p. 169)

The small layer of cosmic dust on the moon indicates less than 10,000 years of accumulation.[7] (p. 26)

The existence of short-period comets indicates the universe

is less than 10,000 years old.[8] (p. 27)

Fossil meteorites are very rare in layers other than the top layers of the earth. This indicates that the layers were not exposed for millions of years as is currently being taught in school textbooks.[9] (p. 26)

The moon is receding a few inches each year. A few million years ago the moon would have been so close that the tides would have destroyed the earth twice a day.[10] (p.25)

The moon contains considerable quantities of U-236 and Th-230, both short-lived isotopes that would have been long gone if the moon were billions of years old.[11] (p. 177)

The existence of great quantities of space dust, which by the Pointing-Robertson effect would have been vacuumed out of our solar system in a few thousand years, indicates the solar system is young.[12] (p. 29)

At the rate many star clusters are expanding, they could not have been traveling for more than a few thousand years.[13] (p. 29)

Saturn's rings are still unstable, indicating they are not millions of years old.[14] (p. 45)

Jupiter and Saturn are cooling off rather rapidly. They are losing heat twice as fast as they gain it from the sun. They cannot be billions of years old.[15] (p. 26)

Among other factors to consider, one is that all the ancient astronomers from 2000 years ago recorded that Sirius was a red star - today it is a white dwarf star. Obviously this view needs to be restudied, with the textbooks in astronomy stating one hundred thousand years are required for a star to "evolve" from a red giant to a white dwarf.

Evidence from Earth

The decaying magnetic field limits earth's age to less than 25,000.[16] (p. 157; 7, p. 27; 8, p. 20; 15, p. 23)

The volume of lava on earth divided by its rate of efflux gives a number of only a few million years, not billions. I believe that during the Flood, while "the fountains of the deep were broken up," most of the earth's lava was deposited rapidly.[17] (p. 156)

Dividing the amount of various minerals in the ocean by their influx rate gives only a few thousand years of accumulation.[18] (p. 153)

The amount of Helium 4 in the atmosphere, divided by the formation rate on earth, gives only 175,000 years. (God may have created the earth with some helium here which would reduce the age more.)[19] (p. 151)

The erosion rate of the continents is such that they would erode to sea level in less than 14,000,000 years (destroying all old fossils).[20] (p. 31)

Topsoil formation rates indicate only a few thousand years of formation.[21] (p. 38)

Niagara Fall's erosion rate (four to five feet per year) indicates an age of less than 10,000 years.[22] (p. 39) [Don't forget Noah's Flood could have eroded half of the seven-mile long Niagara River gorge in a few hours as the flood waters receded through the soft sediments.]

Incredible pressure found in oil and gas wells indicates they have been there less than 15,000 years.[23] (p. 32)

The size of the Mississippi River delta, divided by the rate mud is being deposited, gives an age of less than 30,000 years. (The Flood in Noah's day could have washed 80% of the mud out there in a few hours or days, so 4400 years is a reasonable age for the delta to form.)[24] (p. 23)

The slowing spin of the earth limits its age to less than the "billions of years" called for by the theory of evolution.[25] (p. 25)

Only a small amount of sediment is now on the ocean floor, indicating only a few thousand years of accumulation. This embarrassing fact explains why the continental drift theory is vitally important to those who worship evolution.[26] (p. 155)

The largest stalactites and flowstone formations in the world could have formed in about 4400 years.[27] (p. 27)

The Sahara Desert is expanding. It could easily be formed

in a few thousand years. See any earth science textbook.

The oceans are getting saltier. If they were billions of years old, they would be much saltier than they are now.[28] (p. 26).

Evidence from Biology

The current population of earth (7+ billion souls) could easily be generated from eight people (survivors of the Flood) in less than 4000 years.[29] (167)

The oldest coral reef is about 4200 years old.[30] (p. 39)

The oldest living tree in the world is 4300 years old.[31] (p. 40)

Another factor to consider: The genetic load in man is increasing. Geneticists have cataloged nearly 1300 genetic disorders in the human race. It is certainly reasonable to believe that the human race was created perfect from the hand of the Creator but has been going downhill as a result of our disobedience to the laws established by the Creator. The Bible teaches that we live in a sin-cursed world as a result of Adam's sin.

Evidence from History

The oldest known historical records are less than 6000 years old.[32] (p. 160)

Many ancient cultures have stories of an original creation in the recent past and a worldwide Flood.[33] Over 250 of these Flood legends are now known.

Biblical dates add up to about 6000 years.[34]

The following list of Bible verses speak of *the beginning*:

In 'the beginning' God created the heaven and the earth (Gen. 1:1).

Moses because of the hardness of your hearts permitted you to put away your wives: but from 'the beginning' it was not so (Matthew 19:8).

But from 'the beginning' of the creation God made

37

them male and female (Mark 10:6).

In 'the beginning' was the Word and the Word was with God and the Word was God (John 1:1).

That which was from 'the beginning' ... which we have seen with our eyes ... and our hands have handled, of the Word of life (1 John 1:1).

Besides all of this well documented scientific evidence, let me appeal to your common sense through simple logic. Most proponents of evolution maintain that the universe began with the Big Bang; a gargantuan explosion of all the condensed matter of the universe. The result of that explosion was all the perfectly round heavenly bodies all traveling in precise orbits throughout the universe. So precise in fact that navigation is based on Celestial Mechanics. Look at pictures of the planets, galaxies, etc. from the Hubble Space Telescope and be awed by the beauty and perfect roundness of the planets. If you imagine that the planets of our solar system were the result of an explosion of matter, let me ask a few questions:

Where did the energy come from to bring all of the matter in the universe together and where did all of the matter (elements of the periodic table) come from? Where did the energy come from to cause such an incredibly large explosion? Where is the energy coming from to support the nuclear reactions of these trillions of suns, and moving these massive bodies about in perfect orbits? How did all the complex laws of Physics, such as Gravity or Conservation of Angular Momentum result from an accident with no intelligent design? Lastly, how did an explosion result in such beauty, organization, and perfectly round heavenly bodies? Any explosion I've ever seen has resulted in jagged shaped pieces of destruction.

You may believe Evolution if you choose, but I believe the universe is the evident work of an almighty Creator. By the way, the word uni-verse literally means one (uni) verse, which refers to Genesis 1:1 *In the beginning God created the heaven and the earth.*

Our country's founding fathers affirmed the same in the Declaration of Independence, when they said, "We hold these truths to be self-evident, that all men are created equal, that they are endowed by their Creator…"

The main goal of Satan in advancing the theory of evolution is not to provide answers concerning the origins of life and the universe but to cast doubt on the Bible. When people are constantly indoctrinated by the intelligencia that the universe is billions of years old they doubt the truth of the Bible and are open to the constant misinformation about it.

Attack on the Bible

While Humanism and Evolution have been great deceptions, their purpose is to destroy man's faith in the Bible. Remember, Satan's first great deception was casting doubt on God's Word, the Bible, when he posed the question to Eve, *Yea, hath God said* (Genesis 3:1)? Ever since that time, he has done all in his power to dispute it, distort it, destroy it, and cause people to doubt it. Through Satan's use of human agents, the Bible has been belittled, banned, and burned. Despite ongoing attacks for 6,000 years, the Bible remains and is still listed in the Guinness Book of Records as the best-selling book of all time. It is more than a book. It is God's infallible word which he promised to preserve for us.

The words of the LORD are pure words: as silver tried in a furnace of earth, purified seven times. Thou shalt keep them, O LORD, thou shalt preserve them from this generation for ever (Ps 12:6,7). *The grass withereth, the flower fadeth: but the word of our God shall stand for ever* (Isaiah 40:8).

One of the best historical examples of this is the French philosopher Voltaire. He boasted that within 100 years of his death, the Bible would disappear from the face of the earth. Voltaire died in 1728, but within 50 years of his death, the

Geneva Bible Society moved into his former house and printed thousands of Bibles, distributing them throughout Europe. Today few people read or regard the works of Voltaire, but millions still read the Bible. It continues to be widely published, and people risk their lives even today to bring it to others in countries where it is forbidden.

Some have said B I B L E stands for Basic Instructions Before Leaving Earth. It certainly is everything God wanted man to know wrapped up in one book. One week in Sunday School class a lady came up to me and said, "Have you heard the latest? There is a book out that claims that there are lost books of the Bible." This, like the DaVinci Codes, is just another of a continuing series of attacks on God's Word to cause confusion and cause people to doubt it. These books are heavily promoted, but quickly scrutinized by Bible believers who expose the errors. Unfortunately, these refutations rarely get much press.

Jesus warned, *and many false prophets shall rise, and shall deceive many* (Mt 24:11). The Bible also warns us that in the latter days, *and for this cause God shall send them strong delusion, that they should believe a lie* (2Thessalonians 2:11):

When people choose to reject God and believe the lies of man, He will give them enough rope to hang themselves.

God did however give us simple protection from Satan's deceptions if we will but heed it. God condensed the greatest wisdom in the Bible down to one verse and put it right in the middle of the Bible. The middle chapter of the Bible is Psalm 118, and the middle verse of the Bible is Psalm 118:8. I call it God's Greatest Advice. It is more than interesting that before the middle chapter of the Bible, we have the shortest chapter in the Bible, Psalm 117, and after Psalm 118 is the longest chapter of the Bible, Psalm 119. The middle verse of the Bible, Psalm 118:8 states: *It is better to trust in the LORD than to put confidence in man*. Notice the middle two words of the middle verse of the entire Bible are *'the LORD'*. God put His Holy name in the very middle of the Bible. This is one of many proofs that the Bible is not the work of man. The 40 or so men God used to pen the 66 books of the Bible in over 1500 years certainly did not get together to figure these things out. It is certainly as the Bible states, *For the prophecy came not in old time by the will of man: but holy men of God spake as they were moved by the Holy Ghost* (2Peter 1:21).

This middle verse takes care of man's greatest problem, next to sin, which is <u>trusting the lies of man over the truth of God</u>. It does not say it is wrong to have confidence in man, but rather to trust what God says more than what man says. The Bible says, *yea, let God be true, but every man a liar* (Romans 3:4). A simple application of this verse is to look at what man says, does, and is, from God's perspective, instead of looking at God from man's perspective. If men would heed God's greatest advice in Psalm 118:8, there would be no suicide bombers, no false religions, and people wouldn't blame God for the problems and suffering caused by man and the Devil.

Several years ago, I had a new neighbor move in next door, and I invited him to church. Though he never came he remained friendly and one day came over commenting how much he liked my sports car. I asked if he would like to go for a ride in it and he gladly accepted. I'll call him Joe, though that was not his name. As we rode along, he confided in me that the reason he hadn't come to church with us is that his father was a pastor, who was a hypocrite and didn't practice what he preached. He admitted he was rather unsettled about God, but would be open to discussing it. Later in our home, Joe opened up to me that as he grew up in a preacher's home, he saw great inconsistencies in both parents' lives, and they never had time for him. He was molested as a boy and his father never did anything about it. Later Joe got into drugs, had an overdose, and spent four days in the hospital. He said, "my dad didn't come to see me one time, but if it would have been a church member he would have been there right away." He said, 'To be honest, I hate my father and am angry at God.' I showed Joe Psalm 118:8, *It is better to trust in the LORD than to put confidence in man,* and explained that his problem was that he was looking at God through his father's eyes, rather than looking at his father through God's eyes. The light came on and he readily admitted to that mistake. After a brief explanation of God's love for Joe and God's plan of salvation in giving Jesus as the sacrifice for our sins, Joe knelt beside me at our couch and prayed to receive Christ as his Savior.

When the Bible says *It is better to trust in the LORD than to put confidence in man*, you must realize that it is impossible to truly trust in the LORD without reading the Bible. Otherwise, your confidence is in what some man or woman says about God and the Bible. Instead of people reading the Bible, they listen to what men say about it, whether that be a preacher, theologian, religious charlatan, sports star, movie star, media mogul, or an author who has written some book. People are more willing to listen to people whom oftentimes they don't even know, than to listen to God through the Bible. Why? We don't want anyone interfering with our lives and lifestyles. Did you ever notice that God didn't give Moses the ten suggestions? What God has given to protect us we think is restrictive. Some folks have heard John 3:16, but never heard the rest of the story:

> *For God so loved the world, that he gave his only begotten Son, that whosoever believeth in him should not perish, but have everlasting life. For God sent not his Son into the world to condemn the world; but that the world through him might be saved. He that believeth on him is not condemned: but he that believeth not is condemned already, because he hath not believed in the name of the only begotten Son of God. And this is the condemnation, that light is come into the world, and men loved darkness rather than light, because their*

43

deeds were evil (John 3:16-19).

The Bible exposes our sin, and we don't like that, so we avoid it. However, if we read it and heed it, we are promised a life of God's blessings. A slow reader can read the Bible through in a year by reading only 15 minutes a day. If we would replace TV time with Bible reading time the average person would read the Bible completely through each month. Though in many countries the Bible is not readily available, in the United States of America this is not the case. Though it has been censored and banned in our government-controlled school system, it can be purchased at Wal-Mart for ~ $10. Many times, at the Dollar Store, you can get a copy of the Authorized Version (King James), for only $1. The Devil therefore has taken a different approach in the USA to keep people from the Bible. He has used the old strategy, If you can't beat them, join them. Today there are well over 400 different versions in the English language with many more coming out each year. The problem is that these modern versions are based on a mixture of good and corrupt manuscripts. The Bible says, *A little leaven leaveneth the whole* lump (Galatians 5:9). This means a little *leaven* (corruption), corrupts the entire book, just as a tiny drop of poison in a glass of water makes it all poisonous. There are two different family trees when it comes to manuscripts. The pure line was preserved through diligent scribes, and resulted in the Massoretic text in the Old Testament, which was the same as what Jesus used and quoted during His earthly ministry. The New Testament from the apostles and early church was preserved through a line of Martyrs and persecuted church groups resulting in the Textus Receptus. The corrupt line came from apostate Christianity and the three main manuscripts were the Vaticanus, Siniaticus, and Alexandrian. They account for the 5% difference between the Authorized Version and all modern versions. There are 200 major omissions in the New Testament alone. Let's examine just a few differences:

Isaiah 14:12,15

KJB (King James Bible)

*How art thou fallen from heaven, O Lucifer, <u>son of the</u>
<u>morning</u>! ... Yet thou shalt be brought down to <u>hell</u>,*

NASV (New American Standard Version)

*How you have fallen from heaven, O <u>star of the morn-</u>
<u>ing</u>, son of the dawn, ...you will be thrust down to <u>Sheol</u>.*

NIV (New International Version)

*How you have fallen from heaven, O <u>morning star</u>, son
of the dawn, ... but you are brought down to the <u>grave</u>.*

*I Jesus have sent mine angel to testify unto you these
things in the churches. <u>I am</u> the root and the offspring
of David, and <u>the bright and morning star</u>.* (Revelation
22:16-KJB)

Obviously, <u>Jesus is the Morning Star</u>, not Lucifer. The
connotation of *Morning Star* is of a brilliant Star shining in the
morning sky, while the connotation of *son of the morning*, (as
correctly translated in the King James), is that of a young animal howling at the break of day. As it is talking of Lucifer/Sa-
tan's fall, it is a very different image.
   Who is the *Morning Star* and who is confusing the issue
that it is Lucifer?

   Look at some simple and obvious numerical errors of trans-
lation due to corrupt manuscripts:

<u>NIV NUMERICAL ERRORS</u>

Scripture		KJB	NIV
I Samuel 1 :24	----	3 bulls	3 yr. old bull
I Samuel 6:19	----	50,070	70 [Men]
I Samuel 13:5	----	30,000	3,000 [Chariots]
II Samuel 5:7	----	40 yrs.	4 yrs.
I Kings 4:26	----	40,000	4,000 [Stalls]

Notice how the Trinity has been slyly removed from the modern versions:

Trinity Comparison – 1 John 5:7,8

(**KJV**) *7 For there are three that bear record in heaven, the Father, the Word, and the Holy Ghost: and these three are one.*
8 And there are three that bear witness in earth, the Spirit, and the water, and the blood: and these three agree in one.

(**NWT**) (New World Translation- Jehovah Witnesses)
7 For there are three witness bearers,
8 the spirit and the water and the blood, and the three are in agreement.

(**NASV**) *7 And it is the Spirit who bears witness, because the Spirit is the truth.*
8 For there are three that bear witness, the Spirit and the water and the blood; and the three are in agreement.

(**RSV**) *7 And the Spirit is the witness, because the Spirit is the truth.*
8 There are three witnesses, the Spirit, the water, and the blood; and these three agree.

Do you notice that the three modern versions all leave out verse 7 which is the one verse in the Bible that clearly names the Trinity? They then break verse 8 into two verses so that there seems to be a verse 7. Is this just another Satanic Deception, or poor scholarship on the part of the translators? At best, they are unknowing pawns being used by the Devil to accomplish his ends. A case in point is the example of Dr. Frank Logsdon, Chairman of the New American Standard Version. His testimony follows:

"I must under God renounce every attachment to the New American Standard Version. I'm afraid I'm in trouble with the Lord ... We laid the groundwork; I wrote the format; I helped interview some of the translators; I sat with the translator; I wrote the preface ... I'm in trouble: I can't refute these arguments: it's wrong, terribly wrong; it's frighteningly wrong; and what am I going to do about it. When questions began to reach me at first I was quite offended ... I used to laugh with others ... However, in attempting to answer, I began to sense that something was not right about the New American Standard Version. I can no longer ignore these criticisms I am hearing and I can't refute them ... The deletions are absolutely frightening ... there are so many ... Are we so naive that we do not suspect Satanic deception in all of this? Upon investigation, I wrote my very dear friend, Mr. Lockman, explaining that I was forced to renounce all attachment to the NASV. The product is grievous to my heart and helps to complicate matters in these already troublous times ... I don't want anything to do with it. The finest leaders that we have today ... haven't gone into it [the new version's use of a corrupted Greek text], just as I hadn't gone into it ... that's how easily one can be deceived ... I'm going to talk to him [Dr. George Sweeting, president of Moody Bible Institute] about these things. You can say the Authorized Version [KJV] is absolutely correct. How correct? 100% correct!... I believe the Spirit of God led the translators of the Authorized Version. If you must stand against everyone else, stand." Dr. Frank Logsdon, Co-founder NASB (New American Standard Bible)

Let's examine some changes/omissions that occur in many of the modern versions. For space's sake we will limit ourselves to the gospel of Matthew alone.

MATTHEW
1:25 - (FIRSTBORN) is out. Speaking of the Lord Jesus.
5:44 - (BLESS THEM THAT CURSE YOU) is out.
6: 13 - (KINGDOM, POWER, GLORY) is out.
6:27 - (STATURE) is changed to span of life.
6:33 - (OF GOD) is out. Referring to the kingdom
8:29 - (JESUS) is out. As Son of God.
9:13 - (TO REPENTANCE) is out. Calling sinners
12:35 - (OF THE HEART) is out. Good treasure
12:47 - (VERSE IS OUT) About Christ's mother.
13:51 - (JESUS SAID UNTO THEM and LORD) is out.
15:8 - (DRAWETH UNTO ME WITH THEIR MOUTH)
        is out.
16:3 - (0 YE HYPOCRITES) is out.
16:20 - (JESUS) is out.
17:21 - (VERSE IS OUT) About prayer and fasting.
18: I 1 - (VERSE IS OUT) Tells Jesus came to save.
19:9 - (LAST 11 WORDS ARE OUT) About adultery.
19: 17 - (GOD) is out. None good but (God)
20:7 - (WHATSOEVER IS RIGHT RECEIVE) is out.
20:16· - (MANY BE CALLED BUT FEW CHOSEN) is
        out.
20:22 - (BAPTIZED WITH CHRIST'S BAPTISM) is out.
21:44 - (VERSE IS OUT) About Christ the stone.
23: 14 - (VERSE IS OUT) Woe scribes and hypocrites.
25:13 - (WHEREIN THE SON OF MAN COMETH) is
        out.

48

27:35 - (FULFILLED SPOKEN BY THE PROPHET) is out.

27:54 - (THE SON OF GOD) is a son of God.

28:2 - (FROM THE DOOR) is out.

28:9 - (THEY WENT TO TELL HIS DISCIPLES) is out.

These few examples are the tip of an iceberg but should be adequate to show that there are real deceptions involved in the modern versions. The Bible warns us that there is coming a day when the true Word of God will be kept from the people, as it currently is in many countries. Could the many modern versions help fulfill that prophecy?

In Amos 8:11, *Behold, the days come, saith the Lord GOD, that I will send a famine in the land, not a famine of bread, nor a thirst for water, <u>but of hearing the words of the LORD</u>*:

God did not write four hundred plus different Bibles in English which say different things. He only wrote one and promised it would be pure. Having read through the King James Bible each year and studying it for over forty years, I am absolutely convinced that it is God's Holy Word and the final authority for our lives.

While Satan has many deceptions, these three, Humanism, Evolution, and the attack on the Bible, are certainly representative of his overall strategy. Many of his deceptions and destructive activities are channeled through his devices which are constantly making Science Fiction become reality. These deceptions are carried out in large part by human agents; many of whom are simple pawns, but some of whom are the Devil's disciples. There are many people living today who are traitors to their own families, countries, and planet Earth. They serve Satan for fame, fortune, and most of all power. His many deceptions are enhanced by his various devices.

49

Chapter 5

The Devil's Devices

Invisibility, Disguise, Lies, Telepathy, Technology

Man has long been fascinated with the concept of invisibility, the ability to not be visible to the human eye. In 1897 a science fiction novel was written by H.G. Wells entitled The Invisible Man. The concept has since been incorporated into several television series and movies. What a fascinating concept that man could be invisible to the naked eye, and operate unseen, with access to almost anywhere. Star Trek watchers are familiar with the cloaking device of the Klingon space ships. This made them invisible to the sensors and viewing screen of the Starship Enterprise. That Science Fiction is now reality as our Department of Defense has incorporated stealth technology into aircraft and even submarines. The F-117A Nighthawk was the world's first operational aircraft designed to exploit low-observable stealth technology. The B2 Bomber, the new F-22 Raptor and F-35 Lightning II fighter jets, and even Trident submarines are now employing stealth technology, making them mostly invisible to detection by enemy radar. Scientists at the University of Tokyo have developed an invisibility cloak using optical-camouflage technology. Though imperfect, it shows that maybe the concept of invisibility is not so far-fetched after all.

Our adversary the Devil has had this ability since the

beginning. He along with the millions of other devils that follow him operate in spiritual dimensions that make them totally invisible to the human eye. People who deny God and this spiritual dimension because they cannot see it physically are called Atheists, and God refers to them as fools. Years ago, I remember a 16-year-old athlete I was coaching say, "I'll believe God when I see Him". Unfortunately for this young man that will be far too late. In God's economy seeing follows believing. It is like saying to a fireplace, When you give me heat, then I'll give you wood.

The Bible warns us *Be sober, be vigilant; because your adversary the devil, as a roaring lion, walketh about, seeking whom he may devour* (1Peter 5:8).

Imagine being in a jungle and stalked by a ferocious lion who is totally invisible. The Devil's ability to remain invisible is a great advantage in his war against God's prize creation, man. His stealth operations certainly are a reasonable explanation for the devastation in our society today. Interestingly the rich and famous often have more trouble with failed marriages, drug and alcohol addiction, and suicide than the average person. Many of them frequent psychologists and psychiatrists not realizing they are receiving worldly wisdom from people who themselves lack spiritual vision.

God has made readily available to his children a device that opens a window to the spiritual dimension enabling us to see the invisible. It is called the Bible. Just as the military have developed night vision goggles that enable soldiers to see in the dark, we are able to see clearly into the spiritual dimension through God's Word, the Bible. It states, *as it is written, Eye hath not seen, nor ear heard, neither have entered into the heart of man, the things which God hath prepared for them that love him. But God hath revealed them unto us by his Spirit: for the Spirit searcheth all things, yea, the deep things of God* (1Corinthians 2:9,10). The reason unbelievers have a hard time with the Bible is explained in the following verse. *But the natural (unsaved) man receiveth not the things of the Spirit of God: for they are foolishness unto him: neither can he know them, because they are spiritually discerned* (1Corinthians 2:14).

In addition to invisibility, Satan is a master of disguise and could be nicknamed the chameleon. The image most people have of him as a short little man in a red suit with horns, tail, and pitchfork is as far from reality as you can get. Remember, he was the most beautiful of all God's angelic creation, and nowhere does the Bible say he lost his beauty.

Instead, it says of Satan and his human followers,
For such are false apostles, deceitful workers, transforming themselves into the apostles of Christ. And no marvel; for Satan himself is transformed into an angel of light. Therefore, it is no great thing if his ministers also be transformed as the ministers of righteousness; whose end shall be according to their works. (2Corinthians 11:13-15)

This tells us that Satan and his disciples appear very attractively as God's servants. Unless you understand this truth from God's word you will never be able to come to grips with who the Antichrist is, because he initially appears as such a holy servant of God. Many of today's most popular preachers with the greatest followings are actually Satan's servants. The only way to tell who they are is to know the Bible well enough and examine their fruits. *Beware of false prophets, which come to you in sheep's clothing, but inwardly they are ravening wolves. Ye shall know them by their fruits* (Matthew 7:15,15).

In other words, does their walk match their talk? Have you ever noticed that sin appears very attractive and beautiful? Pornography does not portray overweight or ugly women. Beer commercials don't show a poorly dressed woman who has been beaten by a drunken husband or children crouching in the corner for fear. The devil portrays sin as something to be greatly desired but never shows the results. It is interesting how beer is often promoted by using race car drivers, and yet what NASCAR driver would drink a six-pack before starting the race? Ridiculous! You will likely never see a billboard at a race track showing a father, mother, and children whose bodies have been maimed by a drunk driver, but that is far more honest than the good times shown on commercials. Yes, the Devil is a master of disguise. He appears and makes sin appear as something very different than he and it is.

Another of Satan's most effective devices is telepathy. He has the ability to inspire or place thoughts into people's minds. On one extreme there may be a rock musician like Alice Cooper, of whom it was said that he was possessed. From my former association and later study of Rock Music, I am convinced that Satan is a far greater influence than the average person would be willing to admit. On the same end of the spectrum would be writers of books and movie producers whose products are either overtly occult or even just anti-biblical. However, at the other end of the spectrum might be the little child who lies to their mother. The thought or lie was placed in the child's mind by a devil using telepathy. We are warned in the Bible *to Keep thy heart (mind) with all diligence; for out of it are the issues of life* (Prov. 4:23). A more thorough explanation is found *in* 2Corinthians 10:3-5,

> *For though we walk in the flesh* (physical)*, we do not war after the flesh: For the weapons of our warfare are not carnal, but mighty through God to the pulling down of strong holds; Casting down* imaginations (telepathic input from devils)*, and every high thing* (false philosophies) *that exalteth itself against the knowledge of* God (the Bible)*, and bringing into captivity every thought to the obedience of Christ;*

This is God's provision to thwart the telepathic assaults of Satan. God also has provided believers with spiritual armor complete with an amazing battle sword so that we can victoriously fight the devil. It is explained in the book of Ephesians, chapter 6, verses 10-18.

One of the Devil's simplest but most effective devices is the lie. Most humans by nature are trusting of others. We are gullible and will believe a lie when effectively told. It is alleged that P.T. Barnum said "There is a sucker born every minute." Someone asked how can you tell when a politician is lying? The answer was, when their lips are moving. While there are many honest politicians, we are living in a day when the truth is often hard to find, especially in the political arena. Adolf Hitler was known to say that "if you tell a lie loud enough and long enough the people will believe it". Our media is complicit in feeding misinformation to the masses. During the late 70's and early 80's it was common to see bumper stickers that proclaimed I don't believe the liberal media. The term fake news is popular today, and people are beginning to stand against the propaganda that is often defended as our right of free speech and free press. What used to be known as free press is today controlled by a powerful cabal of super rich globalists, who disseminate information promoting a one world socialist agenda. This is reinforced by the Hollywood crowd and many in the entertainment media. The only area that is worse is the religious arena, especially in Christendom. While there are thousands of faithful preachers of God's Word, much of what people consider Christianity is a cleverly constructed system of lies with the purpose of inoculating people against the truth. The Bible exposes the devil's lies when it says, *for he is a liar, and the father of it* (John 8:44).

One can hardly consider Satan's devices without mentioning technology. Technological advances have blessed society in many ways. Early on, inventions like the telephone, phonograph, electric lights, and television opened up new lines of communication and enjoyment. Today we have progressed to computers, hi-def television, cell phones, social media, virtual reality, etc., etc., etc. God has given people wisdom and knowledge to make life better. According to the Bible, *Every good gift and every perfect gift is from above, and cometh down from the Father of lights, with whom is no variableness, neither shadow of turning* (James 1:17).

God is the Father of lights and in Him is no darkness. He has provided everything that is good for us. Satan loves to take what God has given to bless us and use it to hurt us. Since Sex is such a big part in our entertainment technology today, let's use that as an example. God created man and woman with the desire and ability to enjoy sexual pleasures. Please forgive my straightforwardness, but do you know what the first command was that God gave to Adam and Eve? His command was to be *fruitful and multiply*. As far as I can tell there is only one way to do that, and it is very pleasurable!

> *So God created man in his own image, in the image of God created he him; male and female created he them. And God blessed them, and God said unto them, Be fruitful, and multiply, and replenish the earth, and subdue it:* (Genesis 1:27,28)

By the way, notice that God created them male and female, Adam and Eve, not Adam and Steve. There is no way two men or two women can be fruitful and multiply. God's desire was for man and woman to enjoy the bliss of marriage in the proper relationship: one man and one woman for life. When the religious leaders came to Jesus, they asked him about divorce.

> *And they said, Moses suffered to write a bill of divorcement, and to put her away. And Jesus answered and said unto them, For the hardness of your heart he wrote you this precept. But from the beginning of the creation God made them male and female. For this cause shall a man leave his father and mother, and cleave to his*

wife; And they twain shall be one flesh: so then they are no more twain, but one flesh. What therefore God hath joined together, let not man put asunder. (Mark 10:4-9)

Satan has taken a wonderful relationship that God intended for our blessing and pleasure, and destroyed it through immorality, pornography, and homosexuality (gay lifestyle). The result has been broken homes and lives with single mom's working difficult or multiple jobs to support their children, children growing up with bitterness and no spiritual guidance, and an epidemic of venereal diseases, the most notorious of which is AIDS. The ripple effect of the breakdown of the family unit has been increased crime, suicide, economic hardship and a variety of other ills, too numerous to name. Hugh Hefner of Playboy fame and Betty Friedan of the Women's Liberation Movement, were wrong and Jesus was right.

The devil has used technology, especially in the entertainment media, to indoctrinate and inoculate people against the Biblical truths that will set them free and bring true joy and happiness. Consider the many video games, TV shows, movies, web sites, and text messaging being used to promote the Devil's deceptions rather than God's truth. While we have considered mostly technology dealing with entertainment media, there are many other forms of technology being abused.

If I had to identify the two greatest devices Satan has used in our time, they would undoubtedly be music and the entertainment media. Let's consider the powerful medium of music. Satan is a master musician. As the *anointed cherub*, he was created to be God's honor guard and the song leader in heaven. He literally had musical instruments (*pipes and tabrets*) built into his body (Ezekiel 28:13). He was like a walking musical synthesizer, able to produce incredible musical sounds in his body. There is likely no other created being in the universe that has a greater knowledge of music than Lucifer, who became Satan. Is it likely that when he rebelled against God, that he would use his musical ability against God and His creation? Let's look at just two examples from history. First, the mighty ruler of Babylon, King Nebuchadnezzar, built an image of himself out of gold.

It was at least ninety feet high and he commanded, *That at what time ye hear the sound of the cornet, flute, harp, sackbut, psaltery, dulcimer, and all kinds of musick, ye fall down and worship the golden image that Nebu-chadnezzar the king hath set up: And whoso falleth not down and worshippeth shall the same hour be cast into the midst of a burning fiery furnace.* (Daniel 3:5)

Satan was using a mortal man and the medium of music to entice people to worship a man rather than God. Johann Sebastian Bach stated "The aim and final end of all music should be none other than the glory of God and the refreshment of the soul." God created music for that purpose, and music has always been inextricably linked to worship, even though today it often deifies man, and thereby brings glory to Satan.

The second historical example from the Bible is when Moses was returning to the camp of Israel after receiving the Ten Commandments.

And Moses turned, and went down from the mount, and the two tables of the testimony (Ten Commandments) *were in his hand: the tables were written on both their sides; on the one side and on the other were they written. And the tables were the work of God, and the writing was the writing of God, graven upon the tables. And when Joshua heard the noise of the people as they shouted, he said unto Moses, There is a noise of war in the camp. And he said, It is not the voice of them that shout for mastery, neither is it the voice of them that cry for being overcome: but the noise of them that sing do I hear. And it came to pass, as soon as he came nigh unto the camp, that he saw the calf, and the dancing: and Moses' anger waxed hot, and he cast the tables out of his hands, and brake them beneath the mount.* (Exodus 32:15-19)

Moses returned to camp to find the people given over to idolatry and having a rock festival. Joshua, his helper, said it sounded like the *noise of war*, a good description of rock music. Moses immediately recognized it as the pagan music and dancing that the people had learned in Egypt. When you read the entire story in Exodus, chapter 32, you find that the people were naked, dancing, singing, and claiming to honor God while they worshipped a golden image of a calf. Much of the musical genre' of today contains the same elements which displease God. God is not pleased when we take elements of the world's music (style and beat), and we mix it with a Christian message, claiming to bring glory to Him. That is what they were pretending to do and God was so displeased that He almost wiped out the whole nation of Israel.

While this type of pagan music has always existed in different forms, consider the birth of modern-day rock and roll or rock music. Let me quote from the website of Silver Dragon Records, Rock and Roll - The birth of rock music:

"Rock and roll, like all genres has almost as many definitions as it has fans. Rock and roll generally refers to rock music recorded around the 1950s including mostly southern artists like Bill Haley and Elvis Presley. Rock generally is used to refer to any popular rock music recorded since the early 60's. The word rocking was first used by gospel singers in the south as a slang term for spiritual rapture. A double meaning became evident in 1947 when blues artist Roy Brown's song, Good Rocking Tonight, which he claimed was about dancing was in fact a synonym for sex. Rock music much like blues was limited to jukeboxes and racially mixed clubs and apparently censors were fooled, allowing the song to later be played on the radio to huge success. Many other blues artists followed suit including Wild Bill Moore who recorded a song called <u>Rock and Roll</u> in 1949. Since rock and roll albums were only sold in racially mixed music stores very few white audiences had heard of them. In 1951-disc jockey Alan Freed of Cleveland, Ohio began playing rock and roll for his mostly white audience and it soon became a national phenomenon which would eventually envelop the world."

Alan Freed is generally credited with coining the term Rock and Roll, which at that time alluded to having sex. During a 1993 Oprah Winfrey interview, Michael Jackson, explained the reason for some of his filthy sexual gestures during his concerts: "It happens subliminally. IT'S THE MUSIC THAT COMPELS ME TO DO IT. You don't think about it, it just happens. I'M SLAVE TO THE RHYTHM." The Evening Star, Feb. 11, 1993, p. A10)

It is alleged that there was actually an agenda for our present-day rock music. In the studied opinion of one expert on rock music, the goal of the 1950's was rebellion, creating a division (generation gap) between parents and their children. The goal of the 1960's was immorality, or sexual freedom, promoting sex outside of marriage to our youth. The goal of the 1970's was drug addiction, promoting the use of drugs for enjoyment and escape to our youth. (By the way, in Rev. 18:23 the Bible states, *for by thy sorceries were all nations deceived* (speaking of the end times). The Greek word for *sorceries* is <pharmakeia>, from which we get our word pharmacy, relating to drugs. Drugs and sorceries (witchcraft/Satanism), have always been closely linked. Since the 1980's, the goal has been to promote the occult, leading to literal allegiance to Satan. Many are now following him unknowingly. At rock concerts it is not uncommon to see many even giving the satanic salute. Having grown up through these decades with a strong attachment to rock and roll music, I think this seems rather obvious.

While music is a powerful medium, television combines the power of audio input with the more powerful visual stimuli. Television, which began as purely entertainment, has been a very effective means of advertising and has also developed into a major vehicle for propaganda and indoctrination. While it can be used constructively, it has often been used destructively. Consider some statistics:

According to the A.C. Nielsen Co., the average American watches more than 4 hours of TV each day (or 28 hours/week, or 2 months of nonstop TV-watching per year). In a 65-year life, that person will have spent 9 years glued to the tube.

I. FAMILY LIFE

Percentage of households that possess at least one television: 99

Number of TV sets in the average U.S. household: 2.24

Percentage of U.S. homes with three or more TV sets: 66

Number of hours per day that TV is on in an average U.S. home: 6 hours, 47 minutes

Percentage of Americans that regularly watch television while eating dinner: 66

Number of hours of TV watched annually by Americans: 250 billion

Value of that time assuming an average wage of S5/hour: S1.25 trillion

Percentage of Americans who pay for cable TV: 56

Number of videos rented daily in the U.S.: 6 million

Number of public library items checked out daily: 3 million

Percentage of Americans who say they watch too much TV: 49

II. CHILDREN

Approximate number of studies examining TV's effects on children: 4,000

Number of minutes per week that parents spend in meaningful conversation with their children: 3.5 minutes/week.

Number of minutes per week that the average child watches television: 1,680 minutes

Percentage of day care centers that use TV during a typical day: 70%

Percentage of parents who would like to limit their children's TV watching: 73%

Percentage of 4–6-year-olds who, when asked to choose between watching TV and spending time with their fathers, preferred television: 54%

Hours per year the average American youth spends in school: 900 hours

Hours per year the average American youth watches television: 1500 hours

III. VIOLENCE

Number of murders seen on TV by the time an average child finishes elementary school: 8,000

Number of violent acts seen on TV by age 18: 200,000

Percentage of Americans who believe TV violence helps precipitate real life mayhem: 79%

IV. COMMERCIALISM

Number of 30-second TV commercials seen in a year by an average child: 20,000

Number of TV commercials seen by the average person by age 65: 2 million

Percentage of survey participants (1993) who said that TV commercials aimed at children make them too materialistic: 92

Rank of food products/fast-food restaurants among TV advertisements to kids: 1

Total spending by 100 leading TV advertisers in 1993: $15 billion

V. GENERAL

Percentage of local TV news broadcast time devoted to advertising: 30%

Percentage devoted to stories about crime, disaster and war: 53.8%

Percentage devoted to public service announcements: 0.7%

Percentage of Americans who can name The Three Stooges: 59%

Percentage who can name at least three justices of the U.S. Supreme Court: 17%

Influence of Television

For decades, research and studies have demonstrated that heavy television-viewing may lead to serious health consequences. Now the American medical community, which has long-voiced its concerns about the nation's epidemic of violence, TV addiction and the passive, sedentary nature of TV-watching, is taking a more activist stance, demonstrated by its endorsement of National TV-Turnoff Week.

The average child will watch 8,000 murders on TV before finishing elementary school. By age eighteen, the average American has seen 200,000 acts of violence on TV, including 40,000 murders. At a meeting in Nashville, TN last July, Dr. John Nelson of the American Medical Association (an endorser of National TV-Turnoff Week) said that if 2,888 out of 3,000 studies show that TV violence is a casual factor in real-life mayhem, it's a public health problem. The American Psychiatric Association addressed this problem in its endorsement of National TV-Turnoff Week, stating, "We have had a long-standing concern with the impact of television on behavior, especially among children."

Millions of Americans are so hooked on television that they fit the criteria for substance abuse as defined in the official psychiatric manual, according to Rutgers University psychologist and TV-Free America board member Robert Kubey. Heavy TV viewers exhibit five dependency symptoms--two more than necessary to arrive at a clinical diagnosis of substance abuse. These include: 1) using TV as a sedative; 2) indiscriminate viewing; 3) feeling loss of control while viewing; 4) feeling angry with oneself for watching too much; 5) inability to stop watching; and 6) feeling miserable when kept from watching.

Violence and addiction are not the only TV-related health problems. A national health and nutrition examination survey released in October 1995 found 4.7 million children between the ages of 6-17 (11% of this age group) to be severely overweight, more than twice the rate during the 1960's. The main culprits: inactivity (these same children average more than 22 hours of television-viewing a week) and a high-calorie diet. A 1991 study showed that there was an average of 200 junk food ads in four hours of children's Saturday morning cartoons.

According to William H. Deitz, pediatrician and prominent obesity expert at Tufts University School of Medicine, "The easiest way to reduce inactivity is to turn off the TV set. Almost anything else uses more energy than watching TV."

Children are not the only Americans suffering from weight problems; one-third of American adults are overweight. According to an American Journal of Public Health study, an adult who watches three hours of TV a day is far more likely to be obese than an adult who watches less than one hour.

Sometimes the problem is not too much weight; it's too little. Seventy-five percent of American women believe they are too fat, an image problem that often leads to bulimia or anorexia. Sound strange? Not when one takes into account that female models and actresses are twenty-three percent thinner than the average woman and thinner than ninety-five percent of the female population.[1]

Compiled by TV-Free America
1322 18th Street, NW
Washington, DC 20036

While mentioning only these few, there is no lack of devices which the devil has used to bring misery and suffering to humanity. God warns us, *Lest Satan should get an advantage of us: for we are not ignorant of his devices.* (2Corinthians 2:11) Though Satan also has a large number of devices, he also has a great number of disciples who are employing these devices. We can be street wise and expose them for who they are.

Chapter 6

The Devil's Disciples

In carrying out his plan to destroy the inhabitants of Planet Earth, Satan uses the very beings God created. While many of these have become devoted disciples in various measures of loyalty, most are simply ignorant pawns. The disciples of Satan and the disciples of Jesus Christ are very different. When a person decides to accept Christ as his Savior, he is told to count the cost, take up his cross and follow Christ. There is no deception, but rather truth from the beginning. The devil recruits his disciples through subterfuge. Most who are following Satan's philosophy, morals, and pleasures do not realize that they are following him. Jesus said, *He that is not with me is against me*; (Matthew 12:30). If you are not for Christ, the default choice is the Devil, whether you intentionally choose him or not. He doesn't care! If you are not on God's team by willful choice, you are on the Devil's team automatically by your birth as a sinner. In this chapter however, we will focus on those who do follow the devil by choice. These are those who are knowingly the Devil's disciples. Some are blatant about it like the old rock group KISS, whose name has been rumored to be an acronym for Kings In Satan's Service. Many other rock groups follow Satan blatantly, but many others are very subtle about it and don't want anyone to know where their true allegiance is. This is the case with many of the Devil's disciples who are prominent people in politics, religion, the entertainment and news media, and even education. Many of these have a secret agenda which they constantly deny. That agenda is a one world global society, New World Order, where they think they will have positions of wealth, prominence, and power.

The Bible warns us about them frequently and tells us how to identify those who are not so obvious. Jesus said, *Beware of false prophets, which come to you in sheep's clothing, but inwardly they are ravening wolves. Ye shall know them by their fruits* (Matthew 7:15-16).

These folks will convince you that they are on your side and want to help you. Then they will exploit you. Have you ever dealt with a dishonest used car dealer who seemed to go out of his way to give you a great deal and later you found out you were ripped off? Politicians are famous for promising to help the common man while they exploit us for their own personal gain.

> *For such are false apostles, deceitful workers, transforming themselves into the apostles of Christ. And no marvel; for Satan himself is transformed into an angel of light. Therefore it is no great thing if his ministers also be transformed as the ministers of righteousness; whose end shall be according to their works.* (2Corinthians 11:13-15)

This passage uncovers an important truth about Satan and his followers: Satan does not normally appear as ugly, wicked, and hideous. He mostly appears as good, and helpful, and beautiful. His disciples often appear as ministers of God, and people who seem to be doing good. Al Capone, the famous underworld crime boss, was known to appear publicly at many charity events and make donations to good causes. The same day he might privately crack some people's skulls with a baseball bat or have others gunned down in cold blood. That is exactly how Satan's disciples operate. They are actors and actresses who often portray themselves as saints, but are wolves in sheep's clothing.

The epitome' of this will be the man the Bible refers to as the Anti-Christ, Satan's master diplomat. He will briefly rule the world for a few years before Jesus Christ returns to rescue humanity from this master deceiver.

Let's look at a secret sign used by those worshiping Satan, which identify those who are blatant followers as well as those who secretly serve him. This particular sign is called the Satanic salute and was illustrated first by the founder of the Church of Satan.

The Horned Hand – The Satanic Salute

"The Horned Hand is the sign of recognition between those who are in the occult. . ."1

It can be found by doing an image search on your web browser.

* There are many pictures on the internet which illustrate people or points I make in this book, but are not able to be included due to copyright laws. You may look them up with an image search in your internet browser, which will greatly enhance your understanding. Their titles will be included in a search box.

---

*Image Search-Anton LaVey; horned hand salute; satanic salute. *These searches are recommended for adults only.

Anton LaVey, The Satanic Bible

Anton LaVey, founder of the Church of Satan and author of the Satanic Bible, can be seen displaying the Horned Hand (also called the satanic salute and Il Cornuto) with his left hand, on the back cover of The Satanic Bible.

A little research will show that many of the world's political and religious leaders can be seen giving the Satanic salute. Many of our leading politicians of both parties do likewise. Is it coincidence or have we been deceived by the major players working for world government?

Some may be accidental or photo shopped, but all? Many flash the satanic salute thinking it only means rock on, popular at rock concerts. Satan is a master at deception and confusion and doesn't mind attention through ignorance. Why do we

have such a hard time seeing the obvious? Indoctrination? Deception? Gullibility?

Chapter 7

The Devil's Doom

Before God ever created Lucifer to be the *Anointed Cherub that covereth,* he knew exactly what would happen to him. He knew that he would be lifted up with pride and rebel. So why did God create him then? Well, God could have chosen to create robots or androids who were programmed to only do what was right and were void of a free will. He chose instead to give both the angelic host and the human race free wills, so that we would follow him because we choose to. Our love and obedience would be based on our choice as free moral agents. Can you imagine if our children were robots who could only obey and never choose wrong? Some parents would gladly be willing to try that for a while, but we would have to give up the joy of love and affection from their willing hearts.

God knew what would happen both with Lucifer and then later with Adam, and he already had a plan in place for both. For Adam and the human race, it was the wonderful plan of redemption encapsulated in John 3:16, *For God so loved the world, that he gave his only begotten Son, that whosoever believeth in him should not perish, but have everlasting life.*

For Lucifer (Satan) and the 1/3 of the angels which followed him, the plan was vastly different. *And the devil that deceived them was cast into the lake of fire and brimstone, where the beast and the false prophet are, and shall be tormented day and night for ever and ever* (Revelation 20:10). *The* 'Lake of fire' was not created primarily for man, but the devil. *Then shall he say also unto them on the left hand, Depart from me, ye cursed, into everlasting fire, <u>prepared for the devil and his angels</u>* (Matthew 25:41).

Satan is doomed and damned, with no hope of escape. He is like a dangerous wounded animal. That wound was inflicted when Jesus died on the cross and then rose again three days later. It sealed Satan's fate. No wonder the Bible warns us *in* 1Peter 5:8 *Be sober, be vigilant; because your adversary the devil, as a roaring lion, walketh about, seeking whom he may devour:*

Here is the sequence of his end: He is currently indoctrinating the world against the Lord Jesus Christ and the Bible and preparing them to accept and worship his false Christ called the Antichrist, or the Beast. During the period known as the 7 years of tribulation, the world will ultimately worship the Devil through his Antichrist. Jesus said it will be the worst period of history the world has ever known, *and except that the Lord had shortened those days, no flesh should be saved* (Mark 13:20). Under the guise of bringing peace and prosperity, the Unholy Trinity will bring unbelievable devastation to the earth and its inhabitants through nuclear, chemical, biological, and every other form of weapons. It will truly be a holocaust of unimaginable proportions, where half of the world's population will be destroyed. At the end of the 7 years, God will gather the armies of the world for the final battle of Armageddon. It will be high noon for Satan in his long-awaited showdown with God. Jesus will *return in flaming fire taking vengeance on them that know not God, and that obey not the gospel of our Lord Jesus Christ* (2Thessalonians 1:8). This event is more fully explained in Revelation 19:11-16:

And I saw heaven opened, and behold a white horse; and he that sat upon him was called Faithful and True, and in righteousness he doth judge and make war. His eyes were as a flame of fire, and on his head were many crowns; and he had a name written, that no man knew, but he himself. And he was clothed with a vesture dipped in blood: and his name is called The Word of God. And the armies which were in heaven followed him upon white horses, clothed in fine linen, white and clean. And out of his mouth goeth a sharp sword, that with it he should smite the nations: and he shall rule them with a rod of iron: and he treadeth the winepress of the fierceness and wrath of Almighty God. And he hath on his vesture and on his thigh a name written, KING OF KINGS, AND LORD OF LORDS.

Jesus will slay the armies of the world with the 'sword of his mouth' (God's Word; the Bible), and Satan will be taken, chained and cast in the bottomless pit for 1000 years. The Lord Jesus Christ will then restore the earth to a state of paradise as in the Garden of Eden and will reign on earth for 1000 years. It will be the true utopia man has always dreamed of. At the end of the 1000 years, Satan will be released and lead a brief rebellion against Jesus Christ by those who were born during the millennium but rejected Christ as Savior and Lord. This rebellion will be quickly squashed with fire from heaven and Satan will receive his final judgment, along with all his devils. He will be *cast into the lake of fire and brimstone, where the beast and the false prophet are, and shall be tormented day and night for ever and ever* (Revelation 20:10). This finally and forever ends Satan's reign of terror as god of this world. What a glorious day that will be for the saints of God. What follows next after Satan's doom will be a time of extreme terror for all people who rejected God's incredible love gift of His Son Jesus Christ. Every unbeliever will have their day in court. It is called the Great White Throne Judgment. It will include many people who thought they were Christians but put their confidence in what man said instead of what God says in the Bible.

Jesus said, *Not every one that saith unto me, Lord, Lord, shall enter into the kingdom of heaven; but he that doeth the will of my Father which is in heaven. Many will say to me in that day, Lord, Lord, have we not prophesied in thy name? and in thy name have cast out devils? and in thy name done many wonderful works? And then will I profess unto them, I never knew you: depart from me, ye that work iniquity.* (Matthew 7:21-23)

These are people who made the mistake of following Satan's false prophets instead of God's Word. Their belief was based on emotion and man's teaching, but not on Bible truth. They will appear before God to be judged totally by evidence presented, with no attorney to defend them. In our day there have been several famous cases where people were acquitted despite overwhelming evidence of their guilt. Many people feel justice was perverted by slick attorneys and corrupt judges. That will not be the case in this day. Here is the scenario: *And I saw a great white throne, and him that sat on it (God), from whose face the earth and the heaven fled away; and there was found no place for them (terror in the extreme). And I saw the dead, small and great (every unbeliever, both little shots and big shots), stand before God; and the books were opened: and another book was opened, which is the book of life: and the dead were judged out of those things which were written in the books, according to their works. And the sea gave up the dead which were in it; and death and hell delivered up the dead which were in them: and they were judged every man according to their works. And death and hell were cast into the lake of fire. This is the second death. And whosoever was not found written in the book of life was cast into the lake of fire.* (Revelation 20:11-15)

The books mentioned here are at least two. They are the Bible, which includes the Ten Commandments, and each individual's book of evidence. Each of us has a book in Heaven that is a record of every sin we've ever committed, whether in thought, word, or deed. *For God shall bring every work into judgment, with every secret thing, whether it be good, or whether it be evil* (Ecclesiastes 12:14). That evidence will be presented and no one will be found innocent, for the Bible says, *For all have sinned, and come short of the glory of God* (Romans 3:23). Some people think our good deeds will be weighed against our bad. The problem with that idea is that it is not God's truth but rather one of Satan's lies told by man. The another book, singular, mentioned is the Book of Life, also called the Lamb's Book of Life. It is a reservation book of all who have personally trusted Jesus Christ as payment for their sins, who will never stand before God in this judgment. 1John 1:7 states, *the blood of Jesus Christ his Son cleanseth us from all sin.*

After all evidence has been presented as to the guilt of the unbelieving individuals, the final check is to see if their names appear in the Book of Life. When it is confirmed that their name is not there, they are cast into the Lake of Fire for all eternity, a concept too horrible for us to fathom, because it is permanent.

My earnest desire is that you will not allow the Devil's doom to become your doom. Let me briefly share God's plan for you to be declared not guilty. It is so simple a 5-year-old child can grasp it. First, we are all sinners who have disobeyed God and broken his law. The Bible says, *For all have sinned, and come short of the glory of God* (Romans 3:23). Second, there is a penalty we are due, *For the wages of sin is death* (Romans 6:23). Thirdly, God provided payment by allowing His Son Jesus to die on the cross in our place. *But the gift of God is eternal life through Jesus Christ our Lord* (Romans 6:23). *So Christ was once offered to bear the sins of many; and unto them that look for him shall he appear the second time without sin unto salvation* (Hebrews 9:28). *For God so loved the world, that he gave his only begotten Son, that whosoever believeth in him should not perish, but have everlasting life* (John 3:16).

Lastly, we receive this gift of forgiveness and eternal life by choosing to believe in Christ as our Savior and calling upon him in simple faith and repentance for that purpose. Faith is believing what God says in the Bible and repentance is a change of heart; a willingness to admit our wrong and be willing for God to change our life and lifestyle. *For whosoever shall call upon the name of the Lord shall be saved* (Romans 10:13). When a jailer in Philippi asked the Apostles Paul and Silas, *Sirs, what must I do to be saved? And they said, Believe on the Lord Jesus Christ, and thou shalt be saved, and thy house* (Acts 16:30,31).

When I did this at 24 years old, I simply knelt at my bedside, prayed a simple prayer, and sincerely asked Jesus Christ to forgive my sin and come into my life as Savior. Though I cannot explain it, there was a supernatural transformation that took place, and an amazing life has followed. Satan is doomed and he wants to take as many with him as possible. But God says that He is *not willing that any should perish but that all should come to repentance* (a change of mind and heart).

If you have never yielded your life to Christ, let me encourage you to kneel in submission to God right now and ask him to save you, trusting him alone for your salvation. He will forgive your sins, give you eternal life and his Holy Spirit will become your teacher to guide you into all truth. If you do not have the Holy Spirit in your life, you will have a difficult time coming to grips with the weighty material regarding the Antichrist and False Prophet.

In Satan's invasion and plan to destroy the inhabitants of Planet Earth, his many disciples follow him for the peanuts of fame, fortune, and power. However, he does have two major accomplices that complete his Unholy Trinity. The one is so similar to him in character that God refers to him as the Beast.

Part Two

The BEAST - Antichrist

Chapter 8

The Beast and his Name

The Beast is another name for the Antichrist. Thirty-six times in the book of Revelation the Antichrist is called the Beast. The Bible says there will be many antichrists but one in particular who will briefly become a world ruler at the end of the age. The name Antichrist simply means against Christ and comes straight from the Bible. Most people have heard the term antichrist, but many don't know if he is real or imaginary.

In 1976 there was an academy award winning movie named The Omen, which was about the antichrist. There have been several others dealing with the same topic. From 1999 to 2008 a rock star named Marilyn Manson was performing Antichrist Superstar concerts in preparation for his arrival on the world scene. Marilyn Manson is a male who happens to be a card-carrying member of the church of Satan. An image search will show his card along with the founder of the Church of Satan and author of the Satanic Bible, Anton Szandor LaVey.

While some people have never heard of LaVey, he was a prominent personage with the Hollywood crowd and it is alleged that Marilyn Monroe lived with him for a time. Charles Manson, whose underlings murdered actress Sharon Tate, was also a member of his church. As Satanists are not known for their honesty, there is much information about LaVey that is hard to discern. His relatives also may not be fountains of truth.

*Image Search- Marilyn Manson; Church of Satan membership card.

Another group, Slayer, begins a concert Antichrist, with the phrase, "We all have yet to await the arrival of antichrist". These few examples are just the tip of the iceberg in the promotion and rise of the Antichrist.

There was a time in America that people thought the Devil and the Antichrist were just figments of the imagination in the minds of fundamentalist preachers. Those days are long gone, especially among our youth. I have even been in a few Christian school assemblies where some of the students have flashed the Satanic Salute. Most students probably have little idea of what they are doing and are just following the crowd. That is alright with Satan who doesn't mind attention or worship even through ignorance.

Something unusual is happening in the world today and most people are too busy or apathetic to notice. Satanism and the occult are exploding, while the political and religious leaders of the world are working to bring about a one world government which former President George Bush, Sr. called the New World Order. They already have a person in mind to be the ruler of the one world government, and I believe he is just waiting in the wings till the world has been sufficiently prepared, (indoctrinated). To the surprise of some, this world ruler will not come out of the Church of Satan, but will come on to the scene as a great leader of Christendom. The Bible refers to this person as the Beast or Antichrist. When President Trump was elected, he promised to drain the swamp or the establishment in Washington that was promoting the New World Order and working feverishly and viciously to bring the Antichrist to power.

The apostle John writes, *Little children, it is the last time: and as ye have heard that antichrist shall come, even now are there many antichrists; whereby we know that it is the last time* (1 John 2:18).

This verse, along with three other passages penned by John, are where the term antichrist originates. In 2 Thessalonians 2:3 he is referred to as the *son of perdition*. Thirty-six times in the book of Revelation he is called the *Beast*. In the book of Daniel, he is referred to as the *little horn* and the *beast*.

Is it possible to have a good idea of who the Antichrist will be? Names which have been suggested in the past have included Hitler, Henry Kissinger, Ronald Reagan, Bill Clinton, Mikhail Gorbachev, Maitreya, and many more. These are Satan's attempt to divert attention away from the true Antichrist. The commonly held belief is that he cannot be known until after the rapture or calling out of the church before the tribulation period starts. Most sincere evangelical or fundamental preachers will tell you this is the case. Let's examine carefully what the Bible does and does not say about when the antichrist will be revealed and when he might be known. The relevant passage is found in 2Thessalonians 2:3-10 and says,

Let no man deceive you by any means: for that day shall not come, except there come a falling away <apostasia> (apostasy- defection from the truth) *first, and that man of sin be revealed, the son of perdition; Who opposeth and exalteth himself above all that is called God, or that is worshipped; so that he as God sitteth in the temple of God, shewing himself that he is God. Remember ye not, that, when I was yet with you,*

I told you these things? And now ye know what with-
holdeth that he might be revealed in his time. For the
mystery of iniquity doth already work: only he who now
letteth will let, until he be taken out of the way. And
then shall that Wicked be revealed, whom the Lord
shall consume with the spirit of his mouth, and shall
destroy with the brightness of his coming: Even him,
whose coming is after the working of Satan with all
power and signs and lying wonders, and with all de-
ceivableness of unrighteousness in them that perish;
because they received not the love of the truth, that they
might be saved.

In this passage the antichrist or beast is called by three other names: the *man of sin*, *son of perdition*, and *that Wicked'*. It clearly states that he will not be revealed until he that *letteth* (restrains or withholds) is taken out of the way. This is a ref- erence to the Holy Spirit in the lives of believers, whose influ- ence will be temporarily *taken out of the way* when the true church (all true believers) is removed from earth by Jesus Christ prior to the 7-year tribulation period. To be revealed is similar to revelation, as of Jesus Christ. This means to be pub- licly made known, or simply revealed. It is possible to know who Jesus Christ is before his revelation at his second coming, as all believers now do. My personal opinion is that it may be possible to know who the antichrist is before he is revealed to the world, and I think I know his identity.

When the prophet Daniel was told about the antichrist and his kingdom, the angel Gabriel said, *Go thy way, Daniel: for the words are closed up and sealed till the time of the end. Many shall be purified, and made white, and tried; but the wicked shall do wickedly: and none of the wicked shall under- stand; but the wise shall understand.* (Daniel 12:9,10)

Is it possible that much of the speculation about the anti- christ is simply designed to throw people off the track as to his real identity? Kissinger, Gorbachev, and others like them do not sit in a temple of God and receive worship. These types of suggestions for the Antichrist are just smokescreens. It may surprise you to know that up until 100 years ago there was a general consensus among evangelical leaders as to the identity of the Antichrist. In the next section on the False Prophet, we will try to determine who the Antichrist might be and if he could be alive today.

Chapter 9

The Beast and his Nature

As was mentioned in the last chapter, thirty six times in the book of Revelation the antichrist is called the Beast. The Bible referring to him as the Beast is very revealing. Webster's 1828 Dictionary defines beast figuratively, as a brutal man; a person rude, coarse, filthy, or acting in a manner unworthy of a rational creature. Beasts in general are devoid of any morals or compassion. Their main motivation is to satisfy their hunger and they will attack and devour any man or animal they feel they can overcome. Beasts like a lion can seem very calm and sedate one minute and vicious the next. I have heard several times that the animal responsible for the most human deaths in Africa is the hippopotamus. They look so docile that they are frequently underestimated, but they are fiercely territorial.

Years ago, we took a family vacation out west. At Yellowstone National Park and several other places, we were told not to go near the buffalo. They said that if we get within 100 yards, they may charge and there is nothing we can do as they run at speeds of 40 mph. They also give the appearance of being very docile, but really can be very deadly. Many politicians are the same. In public appearances they portray an image of gentleness and compassion for the citizens they are supposed to serve. In reality many are ruthless when it comes to attaining their goals and protecting their territory. A case in point would be Bill and Hillary Clinton. As president and first lady, they appeared as wonderful people with a sincere desire to help the common man and the downtrodden. President Clinton was a charming and persuasive speaker with sincerity dripping from his lips. As documented in the <u>Clinton Chronicles</u>, during his tenure as governor of Arkansas and then President of the United States, there have been over 50 close associates who have died mysterious deaths. Most were listed as suicides or accidental deaths. The common denominator in all of the deaths were that these people knew inside information about Bill and Hillary that could have been very damaging to their political careers, and several were pursuing actions to make it known. This kind of behavior has not been restricted to just Democrats. While the Democrats and Republicans have very different platforms, they both seem to be getting the same results. Is it possible they are both trying to move us to a New World Order under the antichrist? Some have suggested that Bill Clinton may fit the bill for the Antichrist. It is very significant that Bill Clinton was mentored by the famous Jesuit, Carroll Quigley at Georgetown University, one of the leading Jesuit Universities in our country. How interesting that a professed Baptist would be trained by the militant arm of the Roman Catholic Church.

Over the years there has been much speculation as to who the Beast would be. One of the first candidates was Antiochus Epiphanes, who desecrated the Jewish temple and viciously tortured and slaughtered many Jews. He truly fit the description of a beast. Another beast was Adolf Hitler, who slaughtered many Jews, but also Christians and Catholics. Like Clinton, he was mentored by the Jesuits. While Hitler is regarded as a cruel beast by many in the world today, it must be remembered that the German people regarded him as a savior and hero during and prior to the war. These men are perfect pictures of the Beast who will appear peaceful and yet be utterly ruthless. They will kill their own people, to divert attention, or silence opposition.

In the book of Daniel there are several pictures of the Beast. A very descriptive one follows:

And in the latter time of their kingdom, when the transgressors are come to the full, a king of fierce

86

countenance, and understanding dark sentences, shall stand up. And his power shall be mighty, but not by his own power: and he shall destroy wonderfully, and shall prosper, and practise, and shall destroy the mighty and the holy people. And through his policy also he shall cause craft to prosper in his hand; and he shall magnify himself in his heart, and by peace shall destroy many: he shall also stand up against the Prince of princes (Jesus); but he shall be broken without hand (Daniel 8:23-25).

We learn much of his nature from this passage. First, like a wild beast he is of fierce countenance. However, he is the ultimate two-faced man, appearing friendly and docile in public and vicious in private. He understands dark sentences, which means he is well schooled in the occult. As someone literally possessed by Satan, he has a perfect knowledge of witchcraft. He is mighty in power, but this military power resides in other countries armies. Two examples of this would be the United Nations and the Vatican, who have no armies of their own, but exert subtle political power over others armies. He will destroy in ways of great magnitude, which would likely be nuclear, chemical, biological, or high-tech weapons. His methods will prosper for a time and like Hitler he will practice fraud and deception. It was Hitler who said, "Tell a lie big enough and long enough and people will believe it." He will promise peace and prosperity and then bring destruction and death. The Apostle Paul warned in 1Thessalonians 5:3, *For when they shall say, Peace and safety; then sudden destruction cometh upon them, as travail upon a woman with child; and they shall not escape.*

The antichrist, like his father the Devil, will be a destroyer. He will promote peace to lull people and nations into a false sense of security. Then he will destroy them whenever it serves his agenda. He will think his agenda is to rule the world, but he also will be a deceived pawn of his father, the Devil.

There is not a man or woman on planet Earth that Satan does not hate as we are all made in the image of God, his avowed enemy. He will use the Antichrist in his war against God. There will be two groups of people in particular he will hate with a passion. First the Jews, which are God's chosen people because they brought Jesus into the world, and second those who receive Jesus as savior during the tribulation period. This will be nothing new. Jesus is the focal point of Satan's hatred.

Consider the following chart of Jewish persecution taken from hearnow.org. > Resources > Calendar of Jewish Persecution.

A Calendar of Jewish Persecution

70 A.D. Destruction of Jerusalem 1,100,000 Jews were killed and 97,000 taken into slavery and captivity.

115- Rebellion of the Jews in Mesopotamia, Egypt, Cyrene and Cyprus. Jews and Romans inflicted many barbaric atrocities on each other, causing the death of several hundreds of thousands of Romans and Jews.

132-35- The Bar Kochba rebellion (Bar Kochba was a false Messiah). Caused the death of 500,000 Jews; thousands were sold into slavery or taken into captivity.

135- Roman Emperor Hadrian commenced his persecution of the Jews. Jerusalem established as a pagan city. Erection of a Jupiter temple on the temple mountain (Moriah) and a temple to Venus on Golgotha. Jews were forbidden to practice circumcision, the reading of the Law, eating of unleavened bread at Passover or any Jewish festival. Infringement of this edict brought the death penalty.

315- Constantine the Great established "Christianity" as the State religion throughout the Roman Empire; issued many anti-Jewish laws.

379-95-Theodosius the Great expelled Jews from any official gate position or place of honor. Permitted the destruction of their synagogues if by so doing, it served a religious purpose.

613- Persecution of the Jews in Spain. All Jews who refused to be baptized had to leave the country. A few years later the remaining Jews were dispossessed, declared as slaves and given to pious "Christians" of position. All children 7 years or over were taken from their parents and given to receive a "Christian" education.

1096- Bloody persecutions of the Jews at the beginning of the First Crusade, in Germany. Along the cities on the Rhine River alone, 12,000 Jews were killed. The Jews were branded second only to the Moslems as the enemies of Christendom(Catholic).

1121- Jews driven out of Flanders (now part of Belgium). They were not to return nor to be tolerated until they repented of the guilt of killing Jesus Christ.

1130- The Jews of London had to pay compensation of 1 million marks for allegedly killing a sick man.

1146-47- Renewed persecution of the Jews in Germany at the beginning of the Second Crusade. The French Monk, Rudolf, called for the destruction of the Jews as an introduction to the Second Crusade. It was only because of the intervention of Emperor Conrad who declared Nuerenberg and a small fortress as places of refuge for the Jews, and that of Abbot Bernard of Clairvaux, that the result was not quite as devastating as at the time of the First Crusade.

1181- French King Philip banished the Jews from his domain. They were permitted to sell all movable possessions, but the immovable such as land and houses reverted to the king. Seven years later he called the Jews back.

1189- At the coronation of Richard the Lionhearted,

unexpected persecution of the Jews broke out in England. Most Jewish houses in London were burned, and many Jews killed. All possessions of the Jews were claimed by the Crown. Richard's successor alone, relieved the Jews of more than 8 million marks.

1215- At the IV Lateran Church Council, restrictions against the Jews by the church of Rome were issued.

1290- Edward I banished the Jews from England. 16,000 Jews left the country.

1298- Persecution of the Jews in Franconia, Bavaria and Austria. The Nobleman Kalbfleish alleged that he had received a divine order to destroy all the Jews. 140 Jewish communities were destroyed, and more than 100,000 Jews were mercilessly killed.

1306- King Philip the Fair banished the Jews from France. 100,000 Jews left the country. 1320 In France, 40,000 shepherds dedicated themselves for the Shepherd Crusade to free Palestine from the Moslems. Under the influence of criminals and land speculators, they destroyed 120 Jewish communities.

1321 Jews were accused of having incited outlaws to poison wells and fountains in the district of Guienne, France. 5,000 Jews were burned at the stake.

1348- Jews were blamed for the plague throughout Europe, especially in Germany. In Strausberg 2,000 Jews were burned. In Maintz 6,000 were killed in most gruesome fashion, and in Erfut 3,000; and in Worms 400 Jews burned themselves in their homes.

1370- Jews were blamed for having defiled the "Host" (wafer used in the Mass) in Brabant. The accused were burned alive. Again, all Jews were banned from Flanders and until the year 1820, every 15 years a feast was kept to celebrate the event.

1391- Persecutions in Spain. In Seville and 70 other Jewish communities, the Jews were cruelly massacred and their bodies dismembered.

1394- Second banishment of Jews from France.

1453- The Franciscan monk, Capistrano, persuaded the King of Poland to withdraw all citizens' rights of the Jewish people.

1478- The Spanish inquisition directed against the Jews.

1492- The banishment of Jews from Spain. 300,000 Jews who refused to be "baptized" into the Church of Rome left Spain penniless. Many migrated to the Muslim country, Turkey, where they found tolerance and a welcome.

1497- Banishment of the Jews from Portugal. King Manuel, generally friendly to the Jews, under pressure from Spain instigated forced baptism to keep the Jews. 20,000 Jews desired to leave the country. Many were ultimately declared slaves.

1516- First Ghetto established in Venice.

1540- Banishment of Jews from Naples and 10 years later, from Genoa and Venice.

1794- Restriction of Jews in Russia, Jewish men were forced to serve 25 years in the Russian military. Many hundreds of thousands of Jews left Russia.

1846-78- All former restriction, against the Jews in the Vatican State were re-inforced by Pope Pius IX.

1903- Renewed restrictions of Jews in Russia. Frequent pogroms (massacres); general impoverishment of Russian Jewry.

1933- Commencement of persecution of Jews in Hitler Germany. Inception of the systematic destruction of 6,000,000 Jews throughout Nazi-occupied Europe.

*In viewing the above information, it is very important to understand the marked difference between Christianity as embodied in Roman Catholicism and Christianity known as Bible Believing, Evangelical, or Fundamental. The distinctions should become obvious in the third section of this book. True

Bible Believing Christians love and support the Jews and were not the ones responsible for their persecution. Satan has made it appear that Christians persecuted the Jews in an effort to alienate them, but this will become more apparent later on. The persecution of true Christians is no less significant and is well documented in the famous books <u>Foxes Book of Martyrs</u>, <u>Trail of blood</u>, and in contemporary times by such groups as Voice of the Martyrs.

The Beast is certainly a hideous creature, but he will come on the scene as the compassionate savior of mankind.

Chapter 10

The Beast and his Number - 666

*H**ere is wisdom. Let him that hath understanding count the number of the beast: for it is the number of a man; and his number is Six hundred threescore and six* (Revelation 13:18).

The Beast has a number. It is the number of a man and the number is 666! What God states so simply in the above verse has enormous implications for the entire human race. This simple number of three digits has become infamous in our day and while many have heard of it, few people understand accurately how it will personally affect their life in the future.

In order for the Beast/Antichrist to control every human being on planet earth and enforce their worship of him, he must be able to keep track of them. For most of the last 6,000 years of earth's history this was never possible. Governments have tried to number and control their citizens for years. The United States Social Security System is a prime example. When initially passed in 1935 it was supposed to be a simple retirement system. Now as of 1989, the law states that every child over two years old must have a Social Security Number in order to be counted for a tax exemption. Is it possible the government is more concerned about numbering and identifying each citizen than helping us with retirement? Many governments ultimately seek control over their people, and often use crises or problematic issues, which are contrived or imagined, as their logical reason. This is why our founding fathers were so adamant about the Bill of Rights. They knew the dangers of power in the hands of the few. God strongly dislikes governments having undue control over people's lives because it generally leads to propaganda and ultimately bondage. God's desire is for people to have accurate information and be free. Jesus states in John 8:32, *And ye shall know the truth, and the truth shall make you free. He further explains in* John 8:36, *If the Son therefore shall make you free, ye shall be free indeed.*

This is in stark contrast to the antichrist. God desires our worship, but it must be based on an accurate knowledge of Him and of our own free will. One of the main founding principles of the United States is freedom of worship. Satan knows that if people know the truth, they will not worship him, so he must use deception and coercion. Numbering them is a primary step in gaining control and history records an event where God judged the nation of Israel for doing so. During the reign of King David over Israel, God allowed Satan to provoke David to number Israel. He did this to judge them for their national sin. National sin brings national consequences!

1Chronicles 21:1 states, *And Satan stood up against Israel, and provoked David to number Israel.* 2Samuel 24:15 relates the consequences, So *the LORD sent a pestilence upon Israel from the morning even to the time appointed: and there died of the people from Dan even to Beersheba seventy thousand men.*

Satan has a plan for the Beast to number and control all the people on planet earth, but it wasn't until the advent of the computer age that it became possible. The 666 system that he will use is based on computer code and God says that we can have understanding of it if we have His wisdom. Here is the simple plan that Satan is putting into place by his ruling authorities in preparation for his antichrist:

First, to eliminate real money by getting us off of the gold standard and giving us paper money (Federal Reserve Notes) with no gold backing and so no fixed value. The Federal Reserve Act was passed in December, 1913, while most of Congress was on vacation. This law violated Article 1, Section 10 of our U.S. Constitution. Our gold backed money was replaced with fiat money; Federal Reserve Notes. This is why the U.S. dollar and other currencies are in a constant state of value fluctuation.

Second, to go from cash to check writing, furthering transactions on paper with no real value.

Third, to go to credit cards, where people can literally spend money they don't even have, and then to debit cards, where electronic transactions are immediately deducted from our bank accounts.

The Fourth step is to eliminate cash and go to one card, a smart card, for all transactions. A smart card, chip card, or integrated circuit card (ICC), is defined as any pocket-sized card with embedded integrated circuits which can process data. This implies that it can receive input which is processed - by way of the ICC applications - and delivered as an output. Newsweek magazine, July 31, 1989 (pg. 54) said that smart cards "may make the old science-fiction notion of a CASHLESS SOCIETY REAL." An article in U.S. News and World Report suggests a frightening reason for smart cards. "To keep closer watch on individuals, engineers have devised a forgery proof NATIONAL IDENTITY CARD-THE SMART CARD." In his book, Putting People First, by former President Clinton, he outlines his agenda. On page 22 he states, "All Americans will carry smart cards." (It has been said that these cards have more information about you than even your spouse knows.) The logic would be for convenience, security, to make theft much more difficult, and to eliminate money laundering of illegal activities. Their propaganda never told us of the dangers of identity theft, so...

The final step is to implant the card's financial and personal information under the skin of our right hand or forehead possibly in the form of a small silicon computer chip. All new US passports being issued have a chip (RFID-Radio Frequency ID) implanted, which can be tracked and contains personal information.

The chip may or may not be visible to the human eye. Many people would not hesitate to have a visible mark on their forehead identifying them with their hero, the Antichrist. It would be a badge of honor, much like people wearing a baseball cap on their forehead with the name of their favorite team. Today it is a status symbol to wear clothing with some name on it like Tommy Hilfiger, Hollister, or some other trendy name.

This implanted chip is referred to in the Bible as a *mark in*, not on, the hand or forehead and will likely replace all other cards including our driver's license and the many other cards which fill our wallets. This mark will be linked to the barcode, which first appeared in 1971. In the U.S. it is called the Universal Product Code, which now appears on almost every consumer item known to man. At almost every store today, your purchases are scanned into the computer by item, a total is given, and you may pay in a variety of ways. During the reign of the antichrist, your only option will be to scan the chip or mark in your hand or forehead to make purchases.

And he causeth all, both small and great, rich and poor, free and bond, to receive a mark in their right hand, or in their foreheads: And that no man might buy or sell, save he that had the mark, or the name of the beast, or the number of his name. Here is wisdom. Let him that hath understanding count the number of the beast: for it is the number of a man; and his number is Six hundred threescore and six. (Revelation 13:16-18)

Let's examine the Barcode:
The inventor of the UPC barcode is George Joseph Laurer. In 1971, while Mr. Laurer was an employee with IBM, he was assigned the task to design the best code and symbol suitable for the grocery industry. In 1973, Mr. Laurer's UPC barcode entered the world, and the rest is history.

On Mr. Laurer's former web site, he had a questions page, where he answered various questions about the UPC barcode. On the questions page, Mr. Laurer answered the 666 questions, as follows:

Question #8 - Rumor has it that the lines (left, middle, and right) that protrude below the U.P.C. code are the numbers 6,6,6 ... and that this is the international money code. I typed a code with all sixes and this seems to be true. At least they all resemble sixes. What's up with that?

Answer- Yes, they do RESEMBLE the code for a six. There is nothing sinister about this nor does it have anything to do with the Bible's mark of the beast (The New Testament, The Revelation, Chapter 13, paragraph 18). It is simply a coincidence like the fact that my first, middle, and last name all have 6 letters. There is no connection with an international money code either.

The number 6 is represented by two thin lines in the bar code. For the sake of illustration bar codes generally have two thin lines in the beginning, two thin lines in the middle, and two at the end. In other words, 666.

*Image Search- Bar code 666

One of the first money access cards I ever had was issued in 1984 and has an interesting relationship to the 666 system. It had 6 numbers, 6 - 0's, and 6 numbers in its numeric string. This system is both operational and developing, which is why we are unsure of what the final mark will be. The Bible said that as God's children we could have *understanding*. When a Christian, Dr. Mary Stewart Relfe uncovered and exposed this system, the powers to be became more subtle, changing the numbers string, but all of our cards today are based on the 666 system, in concert with the Barcode.

There is no question that Mary Stewart Relfe, author of When Your Money Fails ... the 666 System is Here, and The New Money System 666, believes the barcode is the *Mark of*

98

the Beast.

"And he causeth all . . . to receive a mark. (Revelation 13:16) In Greek this word mark is *charagma*, which literally denotes a stamp, an impress, and is translated mark. Notice that John did not say that he causeth all to receive a number in the right hand or forehead. This astute prophet could have certainly delineated between a series of numbers, and an unexplained stamp or mark. The same electronic eye which scans the UPC marks [barcodes] will in the near future scan the marks that will be required to be inserted on the body. While some specifics remain vague, of this we are certain: All commerce will be conducted in the near future with a number, a name, or an identifying mark in the hand or forehead. It is my sincere deduction that the *mark of the beast* will not be the insertion of numbers per se on the body, but of vertical lines which will represent encoded messages and digits."[1]

Mary Stewart Relfe, The New Money System 666, 1982

"The Prophet John identified this cashless system of commerce 1900 years ago as one in which business would be transacted with a mark and a number; the mark will obviously be a bar code; the number will be 666; the combination of the two, about which you will read in this book, will be an integral part of the 666 System. . . RECEIVING OF ONE'S OWN VOLITION THE MARK (BRAND) IN THE RIGHT HAND OR FOREHEAD; which I believe will be a Bar Code facsimile incorporating a concealed use of 666, unintelligible to the eye."[2]

The barcode (666) information will likely be on a chip implanted under the skin. The Bible specifically says the *mark* will be *in* the right hand or forehead, not on it. According to Hans Van Doer, Assistant Commissioner for Human Resources and Development in the European Union, they have chosen Cyprus as an ideal prospect to microchip all of their citizens in the next ten years. The chip would be planted under the skin in the right hand or forehead, exactly like the Bible predicts. Van Doer explains that the chips could be instrumental in fighting drug dealing, keeping track of prisoners to overcome prison overpopulation, help monitoring people going through the island's airports as a deterrent to terrorism, prevent illegal immigration, and enable a cashless society where all transactions could be made with the wave of a hand over the scanner. These are all logical security reasons for control.

One company, Applied Digital Solutions, has produced the Verichip and Digital Angel RFID chips for this purpose. RFID stands for Radio Frequency Identification. Florida-based RFID chip maker VeriChip Corporation is in constant touch with the US government to acquire a deal to implant its chips under skin of 1.4 million US soldiers.

Also, Houston inventor Thomas W. Heeter has patented a method to place a mark on a person to enable them to make electronic transactions. While this may not be the mark of the Beast, it shows that people are working toward that direction, either knowingly or unknowingly. Below is a brief of the patent information from the U.S. Patent office:

United States Patent   5,878,155

Heeter   March 2, 1999

Method for verifying human identity during electronic sale transactions:

Abstract

A method is presented for facilitating sales transactions by electronic media. A bar code or a design is tattooed on an individual. Before the sales transaction can be consummated, the tattoo is scanned with a scanner. Characteristics about the scanned tattoo are compared to characteristics about other tattoos stored on a computer database in order to verify the identity of the buyer. Once verified, the seller may be authorized to debit the buyer's electronic bank account in order to consummate the transaction. The seller's electronic bank account may be similarly updated.

Since most all products are already stamped with the UPC barcode, and the system is already operational, the only step remaining is the mandatory requirement for all people to receive the mark, when it reaches its final stage of development. It will become necessary for a person to have the mark of the Beast in order to buy and sell. It will also be necessary for the person to worship the Beast in order to get it. The choice will be simple: pledge allegiance to, (worship), the Antichrist or be killed through starvation or execution. Before this happens, the Antichrist will have to be revealed to the world as the supreme ruler, and before that happens, the true believers in Jesus Christ will be taken out of the world by our Lord in an event known as the rapture. This is promised in the book of Thessalonians.

For the Lord himself shall descend from heaven with a shout, with the voice of the archangel, and with the trump of God: and the dead in Christ shall rise first: Then we which are alive and remain shall be caught up together with them in the clouds, to meet the Lord in the air: and so shall we ever be with the Lord. Wherefore comfort one another with these words. (1 Thessalonians 4:16-18)

Now we beseech you, brethren, by the coming of our Lord Jesus Christ, and by our gathering together unto him, that ye be not soon shaken in mind, or be troubled, neither by spirit, nor by word, nor by letter as from us, as that the day of Christ is at hand. Let no man deceive you by any means: for that day shall not come, except there come a falling away first, and that man of sin be revealed, the son of perdition; Who opposeth and exalteth himself above all that is called God, or that is worshipped; so that he as God sitteth in the temple of God, shewing himself that he is God. Remember ye not, that, when I was yet with you, I told you these things? And now ye know what withholdeth that he might be revealed in his time. For the mystery of iniquity doth already work: only he who now letteth will let, until he be taken out of the way. And then shall that Wicked be revealed, whom the Lord shall consume with the spirit of his mouth, and shall destroy with the brightness of his coming. (2 Thessalonians 2:1-8)

The Lord promised that he would keep true believers, the church, from the wrath to come, the hour of temptation known as the great tribulation.

And to wait for his Son from heaven, whom he raised from the dead, even Jesus, <u>which delivered us from the wrath to come</u> (1 Thessalonians 1:10).
  <u>For God hath not appointed us to wrath</u>, but to obtain salvation by our Lord Jesus Christ (1 Thessalonians 5:9).
  Because thou hast kept the word of my patience, <u>I also will keep thee from the hour of temptation</u>, which shall come upon all the world, to try them that dwell upon the earth (Revelation 3:10).

After the true believers are safely in heaven, the Antichrist will be revealed and not long after, his partner in crime, the False Prophet, will force everyone to receive the mark. The penalty of refusal will be death by beheading and even those who escape will have no ability to buy or sell anything. Starvation will be a grave possibility for them. Those who refuse will mainly be those who have heard the gospel after the rapture and trusted Christ as Savior. Those who heard the gospel prior to the rapture and rejected it will not have a second chance.

And I saw thrones, and they sat upon them, and judgment was given unto them: and I saw the souls of them that were beheaded for the witness of Jesus, and for the word of God, and which had not worshipped the beast, neither his image, neither had received his mark upon their foreheads, or in their hands; and they lived and reigned with Christ a thousand years. (Revelation 20:4)

You may feel that it makes perfect sense to take the mark and all will be rosy. In accepting it you will categorically choose Satan and reject Jesus Christ, God's beloved Son. There are two horrifying consequences with that choice:

1. You will experience the wrath of God poured out upon Christ rejecting humanity during the seven-year tribulation period. It will likely involve a nuclear holocaust with ultimately over ~4 billion people being killed. For those who remain, the seas and water will turn to blood and swarms of satanic creatures will attack mankind with a scorpion like sting resulting in constant intense pain for 6 months. The Bible says it will be so horrible that people will want to commit suicide but be unable to. These are just a few of 21 major judgments, which will be progressively worse. It is important to understand that God is allowing these judgements to happen, but the Unholy Trinity may likely be the actual perpetrators of these horrible events.

2. The second consequence of taking the mark will be to damn your soul for all eternity. There will be no possibility of pardon after that and your ultimate destiny will be the lake of fire for all eternity.

*Image Search- Lake of Fire, Hell

Chapter 11

The Beast and his Notion

The notion of the Beast is neither surprising nor unique. Many individuals have had it down through the years. It is a dream of immense grandeur; to rule the entire world! The ultimate of being number one. Nimrod had it when he built the tower of Babel, but his project failed. He was later cut into pieces by his great uncle Shem and his parts sent throughout the land as a warning against his gross idolatry. Alexander the Great had it when he conquered the whole known world at that time. He died at age 32 after a period of drunkeness. Napoleon, Hitler, Lenin, and many others have had it, but since the time of Rome's domination, no one else has been able to accomplish it. There have been conspiracies throughout history trying to accomplish what the Chinese so boldly proclaimed in the Olympic stadium in the 2008 Olympic games in Beijing; One World, One Dream. Former President George H.W. Bush was the first President in the history of America to boldly proclaim his dream of a New World Order. This is a conspiracy that is longstanding and even our dollar bill has the Masonic/Illuminati symbol of the pyramid with the all-seeing eye, and the Latin words Novus Ordo Seclorum below. They translate to New (Novus) Order (Ordo) of the World (Seclorum). The words Annuit Coeptis mean god has smiled on our undertaking. Unfortunately, it is not the true God who they are speaking of, but the god of this world, Lucifer/Satan.

Satan has worked down through the ages to bring the countries and governments of the world together under his domination through his many pawns in their lust for power and money. His final proxy will be the Antichrist or Beast. God is almighty and sovereign and rules in the affairs of men, but will give Satan some leeway for the world to see his true colors. Satan doesn't want to create a utopia of peace and prosperity as his followers always state. His desire as previously mentioned is to destroy the entire human race, including those pawns of his that foolishly cooperate with him. God has always kept Satan and his pawns in check or else I wouldn't be around to write about it, nor you to read it. When God does allow Satan, through the Beast, to take over for a short time during the tribulation period the resultant destruction and death upon mankind will be unsurpassed throughout history. Jesus said in Matthew 24:22, *And except those days should be shortened, there should no flesh be saved.* The Devil would kill every last man, woman, boy, and girl if he could. Fortunately for mankind he will be stopped short by the Savior, Jesus Christ the righteous.

Chapter 12

The Beast and his Network

There was an old commercial for Verizon Wireless, where they stated what they hoped you would think is obvious; "it's the Network!" Well Satan has developed quite a network down through the years, which will be administered by the beast. As has previously been mentioned, some of Satan's most effective devices are stealth and deception. While there are many people who have researched and found out about the worldwide conspiracy of Satan, most people have been easily duped by the network. As we examine the Network, please keep in mind that what I cover is only the tip of the iceberg, for it encompasses almost every aspect of our daily lives. A few of the areas that the beast has his tentacles wrapped around in his ever-growing network are Politics, Government, Religion, Entertainment, Education, Environmentalism, Military, Media, Business, Witchcraft, and Masonic organizations.

Enter the Illuminati

One of the most important keys in unraveling the mystery of the network is to understand an individual and event that occurred in the early 1500's. The man was Ignatius of Loyola, who was born in 1491. The event was his founding of the Jesuit order in the Catholic Church and his development of the Alumbrados or Illuminati. Illuminati literally means enlightened ones in Latin. His goal in both organizations was twofold: First, to have a one world religion under the Pope, and second, a one world government, also under the Pope. We will give more details on that as we consider the Black Knights in the next section about the False Prophet. Let's fast forward about 250 years to examine the manifestation and activities of the Illuminati in our day. In 1776 a Jesuit priest named Adam Weishaupt brought the Illuminati to America. The United States of America has been the foremost threat to their goals of One World and One Church, thanks to our Constitution.

The Network

With considerable help from Rome and her many agents, Weishaupt methodically developed the network of the Illuminati through two key families, the Rothschilds in England and the Rockefellers in America. They developed several branch organizations most prominent of which today are the Bilderbergers, Council on Foreign Relations, and Tri Lateral Commission. Using the Jesuit strategy of influence through, power, position, money, sex, blackmail, and threat of death or harm to individuals and families, they created a powerful network recruiting people into positions of influence. They progressively gained control of our economy, politics, news media, education, and even much of our military. Through sex and bribes they put many politicians into positions of vulnerability, where they were afraid to oppose the Illuminati's plans. When they did, scandals were brought out in the controlled media, and their lives were ruined. Watergate with former President Richard Nixon is a prime example of this. His demise was engineered by two agents of the House of Rockefeller, Henry Kissinger, and General Alexander Haig.[1] After Nixon was removed from office, the new president, Gerald Ford, nominated Nelson Rockefeller as Vice President.

If people cannot be bought or scandalized, then assassination is often the final option. One example would be Congressman Larry McDonald, a major conservative voice in Congress known for opposing Communism and the New World Order agenda. In the introduction to The Rockefeller File, published in 1976, McDonald states,

"The drive of the Rockefellers and their allies is to create a one-world government, combining super-capitalism and Communism under the same tent; all under their control ... Do I mean conspiracy? Yes, I do. I am convinced there is such a plot, international in scope, generations old in planning, and incredibly evil in intent."

In 1980 Larry McDonald introduced American Legion National Convention Resolution 773 to the House of Representatives calling for a comprehensive congressional investigation into the Council on Foreign Relations and Trilateral Commission. On September 1, 1983, McDonald was aboard Korean flight KAL 007, which was shot down by Soviet interceptors after the plane allegedly entered Soviet airspace. The circumstances and recovery remain a mystery to this day. The loss of much innocent life was evidently just collateral damage, but it sent a strong message to all who would oppose their plans.

To properly assess the influence of the Illuminati today, consider a few of the attendees at their 1999 Bilderberger meeting:

Posted: May 26, 1999 1:00 am Eastern © 2008 WorldNetDaily.com

Clinton and Pope joins Bilderbergers-Secret meeting of global movers, shakers in Portugal. What do Steven Spielberg, Pope John Paul II, Ted Turner, Boris Yeltsin, Bill Clinton and former House Speaker Dennis Hastert have in common? They were among those on a partial guest list of expected attendees to the 1999 Bilderberg meeting in Portugal. Here is list of just a few of the many Bilderberger attendees over the years from the USA:
Hillary Clinton (1997), First Lady of the US when attending, later 67th United States Secretary of State
Lindsey Graham (2016), Senator
Jared Kushner (2019), Senior Advisor to the President, The White House

110

H.R. McMaster (2017), U.S. National Security Advisor, 2017–2018, and lieutenant general.

David H. Petraeus (2015, 2016, 2019), Chairman, KKR Global Institute; 4th Director of the Central Intelligence Agency

Condoleezza Rice (2008), 66th United States Secretary of State

Robert E. Rubin (2016), Co-Chair, Council on Foreign Relations

Bill Clinton, then Governor of Arkansas (1991), President 1993–2001

John Hickenlooper (2018), Governor of Colorado 2011-2019

Philip M. Breedlove (2016), Former Supreme Allied Commander Europe

David Rockefeller, Sr. (2008, 2009, 2011), Former Chairman, Chase Manhattan Bank (deceased)

Paul Volcker (1982, 1983, 1986, 1987, 1988, 1992, 1997, 2009, 2010), former Chairman of the Federal Reserve

Jeff Bezos (2011, 2013), Founder and CEO of Amazon.com

Bill Gates (2010), Chairman of Microsoft

When you add the many members of the CFR and Trilateral Commission, you can understand how powerful and far reaching the network has become.

The Trilateral Commission is a private organization, allegedly established to foster closer cooperation among the United States, Europe and Japan. It was founded in July 1973 at the initiative of David Rockefeller, who was chairman of the Council on Foreign Relations at that time. The Trilateral Commission is widely seen as a counterpart to the Council on Foreign Relations.

Speaking at the Chase Manhattan International Financial Forums in London, Brussels, Montreal, and Paris,

Rockefeller proposed the creation of an International Commission of Peace and Prosperity in early 1972 (which would later become the Trilateral Commission). At the 1972 Bilderberg meeting, the idea was widely accepted, but elsewhere, it got a cool reception. According to Rockefeller, the organization could "be of help to government by providing measured judgment." Zbigniew Brzezinski, a professor at Columbia University and a Rockefeller advisor who was a specialist on international affairs, left his post to organize the group.

Among founding members were Alan Greenspan and Paul Volcker, both eventually heads of the Federal Reserve system.

Funding for the group came from David Rockefeller, the Charles F. Kettering Foundation, and the Ford Foundation.

Sen. Barry Goldwater wrote in his book With No Apologies: "In my view, the Trilateral Commission represents a skillful, coordinated effort to seize control and consolidate the four centers of power: political, monetary, intellectual, and ecclesiastical. All this is to be done in the interest of creating a more peaceful, more productive world community. What the Trilateralists truly intend is the creation of a worldwide economic power superior to the political governments of the nation-states involved. They believe the abundant materialism they propose to create will overwhelm existing differences. As managers and creators of the system they will rule the future."

While never a Trilateral member, President Reagan ultimately came to understand Trilateral's value and invited the entire membership to a reception at the White House in April 1984.

While they say there is no agenda for a New World Order, David Rockefeller boldly admits it in his memoirs:

"For more than a century ideological extremists at either end of the political spectrum have seized upon well-publicized incidents such as my encounter with Castro to attack the Rockefeller family for the inordinate influence they claim we wield over American political and economic institutions. Some even believe we are part of a secret cabal working against the best interests of the United States, characterizing my family and me as internationalists and of conspiring with others around the world to build a more integrated global political and economic structure--one world, if you will. If that's the charge, I stand guilty, and I am proud of it." [2]

A key strategy in the Illuminati plan is to gain control of the USA financially, thereby gaining control of the populace. Our founding fathers knew that financial freedom and political freedom are inseparable. The founder of the Rothschild dynasty, Mayer Amschel Bauer, told the secret of controlling the government of a nation over 200 years ago. He said, "Permit me to issue and control the money of a nation and I care not who makes its laws." Hence today we have a Central Bank, the Federal Reserve, (which is not federal at all), and World Bank, all controlled by the Rothschilds in England and Rockefellers in America.

Quoting from the book, The Rockefeller File, by Gary Allen, "There are several ways in which the Rockefeller Clan controls vast segments of the economy. The first is through the stockholding of the families in the group. Five percent ownership of a widely-held public corporation, according to a 1974 report by the Senate Banking Committee, is considered tantamount to control, especially if your name is Rockefeller. But if we consider only those firms where the Rockefellers own twice that much stock, or have five percent of the stock plus two or more top level management positions, we can put the following companies in the column controlled by the Rockefellers: (The 1975 asset-size rating by Fortune magazine is indicated in parenthesis.)

Exxon (1), Mobil Oil (5), Standard of California (6),

Standard of Indiana (13), International Harvester (26), In-land Steel (78), Marathon Oil (60), Quaker Oats (163), Wheeling-Pittsburgh Steel (194), Freeport Sulphur, and International Basic Economy Corporation."[3]

"Another way the Rockefellers control vast segments of our economy is through trust departments through at least two of its megabanks, First National City Bank (City Bank), and Chase Manhattan Bank. Chase's trust department alone controls the single largest block of stock in 21 major American corporations. Among these are United Airlines, Northwest Airlines, and Atlantic Richfield Oil, along with 18 other multimillion dollar firms."

Other corporations controlled by the Rockefellers through other financial institutions (with the 1975 Fortune rating in parentheses) include:

IBM (9), Mobil (5), Texaco (4), IT&T (10), Westing-house (19), Boeing (39), International Paper (56), Minnesota Mining & Manufacturing (59), Sperry Rand (70), Xerox (41), National Cash Register (97), National Steel (64), American Home Products (92), Pfizer (130), Avon (159), and Merck (152).[4]

Transportation companies under Rockefeller influence (with 1975 Fortune ranking for transportation corporations noted in parenthesis) are as follows:

Penn Central (T3), TWA (T1), Eastern Airlines (T8), United Airlines (T2), National Airlines (T26), Delta (T13), Braniff (T19), Northwest Airlines (T18), and Consolidated Freightways (T17).[5]

Other major corporations in which the Rockefellers have significant influence, either direct or indirect, but not enough to prove working control, are:

AT&T (U1), Motorola (149), Safeway (R-2), Honey-well (68), General Foods (58), Hewlett-Packard (225), and Burlington Industries (86).[6]

"This relates to yet another method for economic control is interlocking directorates. An interlocking directorate exists between two companies when a member of the board of directors of one company also sits on the board of directors of the other company. This was theoretically outlawed by Section 8 of the Clayton Act, which says that no person shall be a director at one time in any two or more competing companies. This law is enforced almost as strictly as the one against jaywalking in New York City. Tracing all of the interlocks among the Rockefeller Group's representatives on various boards of directors is a challenge that would reduce even Einstein to a babbling idiot. Just a few of the major corporations not previously mentioned that have interlocking-directorate ties with the Rockefeller Groups include:

Allied (Chemical) (85),. Anaconda Copper (118), DuPont (17), Monsanto(43), Olin Mathison (161), Borden (47), National Distillers (185), Shell (14), Gulf (7), Union Oil (34), Dow (27), Celanese (101), Pittsburgh Plate Glass (113), Cities Service (61), Stauffer Chemical (233), Continental Oil (16), Union Carbide (22), American Cyanamid (107), American Motors (93), Bendix (77), Chrysler (11), C.LT. Financial (F9), S. S. Kresge (R5), and R. H. Macy (R27)."[7]

This information dates back to 1975, but today we are seeing the end result of Rockefeller controlled corporations being used to destroy our economy. Take Lehman Brothers as an example. This was one of the earliest Illuminati footholds through which a power base was established. They continually fronted money to business ventures furthering their cause, and whether through faulty management or careful planning they declare bankruptcy and asked the US citizens to bail them out. This situation, the Freddie Mac and Fannie Mae scams, and the oil price scam are nothing but a great transfer of wealth from the pockets of the hard-working American people into the pockets of the traitorous conspirators. They are destroying America from within, and bringing the people into financial, then political, then spiritual bondage.

This network not only has great influence in the financial and political arenas, but has gained substantial control over our news and entertainment industry, our educational system, the military, religion, and just about every aspect of our life. Let me sight a few examples. As a young teacher all I was familiar with was our progressive education philosophy and methods, which were consistently producing poor results in our schools. After becoming a Christian, I became aware that our country had a traditional approach and philosophy of education for the first 150 years, which resulted in us having one of the highest standards of education in the world. The John Dewey era, as previously mentioned, changed all of that. Columnist John Leo wrote: "Schools are flooded with progressive experiments and social agendas that either go down in flames or crowd out actual learning. Cooperative learning, the politics of identity, outcome-based education, and history as group therapy all fall into this category. An emphasis on egalitarianism in the classroom often has strange effects, making some teachers suspicious of achievement and any knowledge that contributes to inequality." Some teachers now refer to themselves as facilitators because they believe teaching is an expression of dominance."

A front-page article appeared in USA Today newspaper which stated, "90 million can barely read, write." The article went on to state "Almost half of U.S. adults have very limited reading and writing skills, although most say they are able to read and write English well or very well, an Education Department report out today shows."[8] Achieving success in education is no great secret as fundamental principles and methods have succeeded for most of our country's history as well as for thousands of years spanning many civilizations. As a teacher concerned about our failing system, I realized that our educational leadership in America were either really ignorant of these methods, or, they had an agenda. I came to the conclusion that they have an agenda and it is to establish a one world socialist government, which was John Dewey's goal. Another example relating to the news media: having lived in a mid-size city in Florida, we had one newspaper. Despite the fact that our community had always been a very conservative Bible belt area with traditional values, our newspaper constantly promoted the very opposite in its reporting. It has even rejected letters to the editor that conflict with its amoral and political viewpoints. Not surprising is that the newspaper is owned by the NY Times in New York. It is a major source of frustration to many people of faith in the community whose voices and values have been effectively repressed.

The first Amendment to our Constitution states: "Congress shall make no law respecting an establishment of religion, or prohibiting the free exercise thereof; or abridging the freedom of speech, or of the press; or the right of the people peaceably to assemble, and to petition the Government for a redress of grievances."

Our founding fathers were adamant about the importance of a free press and yet today we have a controlled press and often it seems the only ones who are guaranteed free speech are the pornographers and the movie industry. Anyone of reasonable intelligence can understand the simple language of the first amendment, and yet the practice of our judges and government officials is to rule contrary to the document they are sworn to uphold, the United States Constitution. Take the first provision of this amendment: "Congress shall make no law respecting an establishment of religion, or prohibiting the free exercise thereof;" This is rarely quoted as it tells government that they have no right to make laws in regard to (respecting) religion (which from our founding documents obviously refers to Christianity, not Satanism, Buddhism, or Islam). It simply says that government should keep their hands off the church. Nowhere does it say that the church has no right to influence politics or government. There has been a barrage of rulings in my lifetime where the government is constantly trying to restrict the influence of the Christian churches and remove all references to the Bible, Christ, and Christianity from our country. Obvious examples are removing nativity scenes from public displays, removing the Ten Commandments, prayer and the Bible, from schools and public buildings, and even the attempt to remove the motto In God we Trust from our pledge of allegiance and money. You may feel that these violate the separation of church and state! It is vitally important for Americans to note that the phrase "separation of church and state" is not a part of any of our founding documents. It is not in the Constitution or the Bill of Rights! It was a phrase written by Thomas Jefferson to a pastor who was concerned about having a state church like they came from in England. Jefferson was reassuring him that government would not take over religion or restrict its free exercise. This phrase from a personal, not official, letter has been taken out of context and used to accomplish the very opposite of what our founding fathers clearly intended in the Constitution. Is someone working on an agenda opposing our Christian foundations of government? You decide. It is your eternity they are manipulating.

Let's give one last example realizing that there have been many complete books written about each of these individual topics. The movie industry, another key player in the network, has changed dramatically since I was a boy. When the movie Gone with the Wind came out in 1939 and Clark Gable uttered one curse word at the end, "Frankly my dear, I don't give a damn", there was quite an uproar over the use of one curse word. Movie standards at that time were very strict. Sexual overtones and immodesty were shunned at that time. Now push the fast forward button on your remote to 2020. Hollywood, through movies and videos constantly promote immorality, nudity, obscene language, and two of the most popular themes of late is the occult and the sodomite (gay) lifestyles. While many have occult themes understood only by those familiar with witchcraft and Satanism, many TV series like Buffy and Charmed were blatantly occult.

Sports are a great recreation and watching them is a wonderful diversion. Many people agree that sports have moved from being a diversion to a distraction, occupying a great amount of the average American's time and anesthetizing us from being involved in the problems of our day. Why are sporting events being used to promote beer and now rock music? Honestly, what do Budweiser and NASCAR have in common? What NASCAR driver would slurp down a few beers before the big race? Or what NFL quarterback would have a few beers before the game to loosen up? Yet sports are being used to promote one of the most destructive of drugs; alcohol, a substance known to be toxic to the body, and destructive to society. Why all of a sudden have sporting events been promoting country/rock singers and having mini concerts during halftime or during commercial breaks? Though most people have been desensitized to the negative influence of rock music, we need to stop and consider it objectively. From its birth and evolution, it has been associated with rebellion, immorality, drugs, and now blatant Satanism. Personally, having grown up loving rock music, I was never aware of its dark side until someone made me stop and think. Its results speak for itself as it has been named as a factor in numerous suicides, murders, and other crimes. Thomas W. Wedge is one of the leading experts in the United States on Satanism and Satanic crimes. He has written a book entitled The Satan Hunter, to assist law enforcement agencies in dealing with these often-hideous crimes. In giving a seminar on the rise of Satanic crimes to law enforcement personnel in Fitzgerald, Georgia he made a statement that stunned many of the officers who came from as far away as Daytona Beach, Florida. According to a friend in attendance, Mr. Wedge asserted that one of the main reasons for the growth of Satanism and related crimes in America was the prominence of rock music. Another expert on the Occult is David Benoit. In his well-researched video Occult Tendencies in Rock Music, he relates the story of a known practicing witch being interviewed on a talk show. The witch said that as a member of the Church of Satan, she pays tithes to her church, which is an offering of 10% of her income. She said that 90%

of that money goes to promote and support rock music, as the Church of Satan feels that is the most effective way to reach people for the Devil.

If any of my surmising seems absurd, consider the Communist Goals for American Takeover. For brevity, I will not include all 45 goals, but a few relating to what I have already shared.

Communist Goals for American Takeover
Communist Goals (1963)
Congressional Record--Appendix, pp. A34-A35
January 10, 1963

1. U.S. acceptance of coexistence as the only alternative to atomic war. (Disarmament)
4. Permit free trade between all nations regardless of Communist affiliation and regardless of whether or not items could be used for war.
7. Grant recognition of Red China. Admission of Red China to the U.N.
11. Promote the U.N. as the only hope for mankind. If its charter is rewritten, demand that it be set up as a one-world government with its own independent armed forces.
15. Capture one, or both, of the political parties in the United States.
16. Use technical decisions of the courts to weaken basic American institutions by claiming their activities violate civil rights.
17. Get control of the schools. Use them as transmission belts for socialism and current Communist propaganda. Soften the curriculum. Get control of teachers' associations. Put the party line in textbooks.
20. Infiltrate the press. Get control of book-review assignments, editorial writing, policymaking positions.
21. Gain control of key positions in radio, TV, and motion pictures.

120

24. Eliminate all laws governing obscenity by calling them "censorship" and a violation of free speech and free press.

25. Break down cultural standards of morality by promoting pornography and obscenity in books, magazines, motion pictures, radio, and TV.

26. Present homosexuality, degeneracy and promiscuity as "normal, natural, healthy."

27. Infiltrate the churches and replace revealed religion with "social" religion. Discredit the Bible and emphasize the need for intellectual maturity which does not need a "religious crutch."

28. Eliminate prayer or any phase of religious expression in the schools on the ground that it violates the principle of "separation of church and state."

29. Discredit the American Constitution by calling it inadequate, old-fashioned, out of step with modern needs, a hindrance to cooperation between nations on a worldwide basis.

30. Discredit the American Founding Fathers. Present them as selfish aristocrats who had no concern for the "common man."

32. Support any socialist movement to give centralized control over any part of the culture -- education, social agencies, welfare programs, mental health clinics, and etcetera.

37. Infiltrate and gain control of big business.

40. Discredit the family as an institution. Encourage promiscuity and easy divorce.

41. Emphasize the need to raise children away from the negative influence of parents. Attribute prejudices, mental blocks and retarding of children to suppressive influence of parents.

44. Internationalize the Panama Canal.

45. Repeal the Connally reservation so the United States cannot prevent the World Court from seizing

jurisdiction over domestic problems. Give the World Court jurisdiction over nations and individuals alike.

These along with the following give an accurate picture of the grave danger our country is in due to traitors in government and our public institutions.

The 10 PLANKS stated in the Communist Manifesto and some of their American counterparts are...

1. Abolition of private property and the application of all rents of land to public purposes.
Americans do these with actions such as the 14th Amendment of the U.S. Constitution (1868), and various zoning, school & property taxes. Also, the Bureau of Land Management (Zoning laws are the first step to government property ownership)

2. A heavy progressive or graduated income tax.
Americans know this as misapplication of the 16th Amendment of the U.S. Constitution, 1913, The Social Security Act of 1936.; Joint House Resolution 192 of 1933; and various State "income" taxes. We call it "paying your fair share".

3. Abolition of all rights of inheritance.
Americans call it Federal & State estate Tax (1916); or reformed Probate Laws, and limited inheritance via arbitrary inheritance tax statutes.

4. Confiscation of the property of all emigrants and rebels.
Americans call it government seizures, tax liens, Public "law" 99-570 (1986); Executive order 11490, sections 1205, 2002 which gives private land to the Department of Urban Development; the imprisonment of "terrorists" and those who speak out or write against the "government" (1997 Crime/Terrorist Bill); or the IRS confiscation of property without due process. Asset forfeiture laws are used by DEA, IRS, ATF etc...).

5. Centralization of credit in the hands of the state, by means of a national bank with State capital and an exclusive monopoly.

Americans call it the Federal Reserve which is a privately-owned credit/debt system allowed by the Federal Reserve act of 1913. All local banks are members of the Fed system, and are regulated by the Federal Deposit Insurance Corporation (FDIC) another privately-owned corporation. The Federal Reserve Banks issue Fiat Paper Money and practice economically destructive fractional reserve banking.

6. Centralization of the means of communications and transportation in the hands of the State.

Americans call it the Federal Communications Commission (FCC) and Department of Transportation (DOT) mandated through the ICC act of 1887, the Commissions Act of 1934, The Interstate Commerce Commission established in 1938, The Federal Aviation Administration, Federal Communications Commission, and Executive orders 11490, 10999, as well as State mandated driver's licenses and Department of Transportation regulations.

7. Extension of factories and instruments of production owned by the state, the bringing into cultivation of waste lands, and the improvement of the soil generally in accordance with a common plan.

Americans call it corporate capacity, The Desert Entry Act and The Department of Agriculture... Thus read "controlled or subsidized" rather than "owned"... This is easily seen in these as well as the Department of Commerce and Labor, Department of Interior, the Environmental Protection Agency, Bureau of Land Management, Bureau of Reclamation, Bureau of Mines, National Park Service, and the IRS control of business through corporate regulations.

8. Equal liability of all to labor. Establishment of

industrial armies, especially for agriculture.

Americans call it Minimum Wage and slave labor like dealing with our Most Favored Nation trade partner; i.e. Communist China. We see it in practice via the Social Security Administration and The Department of Labor. The National debt and inflation caused by the communal bank has caused the need for a two "income" family. Woman in the workplace since the 1920's, the 19th amendment of the U.S. Constitution, the Civil Rights Act of 1964, assorted Socialist Unions, affirmative action, the Federal Public Works Program and of course Executive order 11000.

9. Combination of agriculture with manufacturing industries, gradual abolition of the distinction between town and country, by a more equitable distribution of population over the country.

Americans call it the Planning Reorganization act of 1949 , zoning (Title 17 1910-1990) and Super Corporate Farms, as well as Executive orders 11647, 11731 (ten regions) and Public "law" 89-136. These provide for forced relocations and forced sterilization programs, like in China.

10. Free education for all children in public schools. Abolition of children's factory labor in its present form. Combination of education with industrial production.

* Please understand that the information given above is not from the author but from the Congressional Record in the year 1963.

Many older Americans realize that many of these goals are already in place and many others are current battlegrounds we are fighting. To those few Americans who have read our Constitution, it is very obvious that the communist goals are in direct opposition to it. Our foundations have been destroyed through lack of knowledge. It is the opinion of this author that communism is still alive and well but is nothing more than a network tool of the coming Beast/Antichrist to bring in his kingdom. It does reveal a lot about his goals and methods and we always need to keep in mind that the power behind it all is Satan.

126

Chapter 13

The Beast and his Nemesis

According to Webster's Seventh Collegiate Dictionary, a Nemesis is defined as "one that inflicts retribution or vengeance", or "a formidable and victorious rival". Both of these definitions are perfectly appropriate with regards to the person who will ultimately confront the Beast, the False Prophet, and the Devil. They will face their nemesis through eyes full of terror and know that they made an enormous mistake.

Just as Al Capone had a nemesis by the name of Elliott Ness, so will the Beast have an opponent. His reign will be relatively short-lived before he will meet up with his Nemesis. To give a couple of parallel examples to ponder: Al Capone, America's most famous gangster, only ruled Chicago's crime syndicate for about 10 years. The reign of Adolf Hitler lasted a mere 12 years. Compared to many kings and rulers throughout history, that is very brief. For instance, King David reigned over Israel for 40 years. During WWII, things were going very well for Hitler but then Japanese Emperor Hirohito attacked the United States at Pearl Harbor, bringing us into the war. When Hitler heard that news, his response to his advisors was, "I wish he wouldn't have done that". Having the United States as his nemesis limited Hitler's reign of terror to 12 years, and ended with his humiliating defeat and suicide.

Despite the millennia of planning and scheming to bring the world ruler known as the antichrist into power, his reign will last only 7 brief years. In those brief 7 years the Antichrist, under the empowerment of Satan, will have devastated the earth leaving over half of its inhabitants dead. His Nemesis is none other than the Lord Jesus Christ and he will confront the

Beast at the very height of the Battle of Armageddon. The armies of the world will be gathered in the valley of Megiddo, called in the Hebrew tongue Armageddon. While they will be fighting amongst themselves in rebellion against the Beast, they will be interrupted by the entrance of an army from heaven. The Bible gives a very descriptive account of this awesome event which is known as the Second Coming of Christ.

The Beast and the armies of the world, with all of their ultra-sophisticated, high-tech weapons, will be absolutely powerless against the Lord Jesus Christ when he appears to mete out divine retribution. Jesus will be the formidable and victorious rival; the Nemesis. For those who are unsure that this mighty King of Kings and Lord of Lords is Jesus Christ, it is made clear in several other passages in the Bible. In 1 Timothy 6:14,15, the Apostle Paul writes, *That thou keep this commandment without spot, unrebukable, until the appearing of our Lord Jesus Christ: Which in his times he shall shew, who is the blessed and only Potentate, the King of kings, and Lord of lords;*

Also, when the above text says, *his name is called The Word of God,* he is identified in John, chapter 1. Writing about Jesus, John refers to him as *the Word* in verse 1. *In the beginning was the Word, and the Word was with God, and the Word was God.*

He then speaks of his incarnation (virgin birth) in verse 14, *And the Word was made flesh, and dwelt among us, and we beheld his glory, the glory as of the only begotten of the Father, full of grace and truth.* Also, in 1 John 5:7, *For there are three that bear record in heaven, the Father, the Word, and the Holy Ghost: and these three are one.* This verse speaks of the Trinity of the Father, Son (the Word), and the Holy Ghost. An interesting side note, as has been previously stated, in Satan's attempt to confuse the identity of Jesus Christ and his place in the Trinity as Almighty God, this verse has been removed from most of the modern versions of the Bible.

128

The account of the Second Coming is in stark contrast to Christ's first coming when he appeared as a babe in a manger. He grew up as a suffering savior; a sacrificial lamb who was crucified on the cross to pay for our sins. Prior to his death, he rode into Jerusalem on a donkey as a picture of a humble servant. During his second coming to rescue planet earth from the Beast, Jesus appears on a white horse, a symbol of a conquering king. These two contrasting pictures of the Messiah are the reason many Jews have been confused as to who the Messiah is. Had they simply read the Old Testament, and the many prophecies about the Messiah, they would know that Jesus Christ is the only one to fit the prophecies. Instead of studying for themselves, they simply believed their religious leaders, the very ones whose ancestors slew the Messiah.

The prophet Isaiah wrote:

Isaiah 53:1 *Who hath believed our report? and to whom is the arm of the LORD revealed?* [Isaiah 51:9; John 12:38; Romans 1:16; 10:16; 1Corinthians 1:18]
2 *For he shall grow up before him as a tender plant, and as a root out of a dry ground: he hath no form nor comeliness; and when we shall see him, there is no beauty that we should desire him.* [Isaiah 11:1; 52:14; Mark 9:12]
3 *He is despised and rejected of men; a man of sorrows, and acquainted with grief: and we hid as it were our faces from him; he was despised, and we esteemed him not.* [Psalm 22:6; Isaiah 49:7; John 1:10-11; Hebrews 4:15]
4 *Surely he hath borne our griefs, and carried our sorrows: yet we did esteem him stricken, smitten of God, and afflicted.* [Matthew 8:17; Hebrews 9:28; 1Peter 2:24]
5 *But he was wounded for our transgressions, he was bruised for our iniquities: the chastisement of our peace was upon him; and with his stripes we are*

healed. [Romans 4:25; 1Corinthians 5:13; 1Peter 2:24; 3:18]

6 *All we like sheep have gone astray; we have turned every one to his own way; and the LORD hath laid on him the iniquity of us all.* [Psalms 119:176; 1Peter 2:25]

7 *He was oppressed, and he was afflicted, yet he opened not his mouth: he is brought as a lamb to the slaughter, and as a sheep before her shearers is dumb, so he openeth not his mouth.* [Matthew 26:63; 27:12,14; Mark 14:61; 15:5; Acts 8:32; 1Peter 2:23]

I have placed additional references in between the verses, so that those eager to do the research can gain more insight.

The God/man who came the first time in humility and suffering will manifest his true position and nature at his second coming. He will be the hero and Savior of all His followers who were oppressed by the beast and all of his followers.

The Bible further explains the confrontation between the Beast and his nemesis, when it states,

And to you who are troubled rest with us, when the Lord Jesus shall be revealed from heaven with his mighty angels, in flaming fire taking vengeance on them that know not God, and that obey not the gospel of our Lord Jesus Christ: Who shall be punished with everlasting destruction from the presence of the Lord, and from the glory of his power (2Thessalonians 1:7-9).

At the conclusion of the Battle of Armageddon when Jesus returns and slays the armies of the world, the Bible says in Revelation 14:20 that the blood in the valley would be to *the horse bridles as far as a thousand and six hundred furlongs*, which is about two hundred miles. To be honest, though I believed this Bible passage by faith, I must admit that I had a hard time

130

understanding how there could be so much blood in that vast expanse. Then in 2008 when I visited Israel and the valley of Armageddon, God was gracious to give me understanding, which proved to be rather simple. In the visitor center was a topographic map of the valley. The map revealed that there are channels in the midst of the valley similar to a stream bed at the bottom of the lake. It is now not difficult to imagine the blood from hundreds of millions of soldiers draining into these channels and reaching to the height of a horse bridles. It reminded me that often people doubt God and the Bible because we are mortal creatures who do not understand an infinite God and his ways.

Such carnage will result from people choosing to believe a smooth-talking world dictator rather than God. Despite this beast being the most powerful Satan possessed man who ever lived, he will only be in power for 7 years, 5 years shorter than Hitler. It is said that Hitler was responsible for the death of at least 23 million people. In the brief 7-year reign of the Antichrist, known to Bible believers as the Tribulation period, there will be about 4 billion people killed. Fortunately, the beast does have a nemesis who will stop him, and his name is Jesus Christ. For that I am eternally grateful. The beast will finally be confronted by Jesus Christ, and face his eternal night.

Chapter 14

The Beast and his Night

The beast has a future which is black. That future is eternal night.

The Beast and his False Prophet will be taken alive and cast into the lake of fire. All of his followers will be slain and cast into hell, which is different than the lake of fire. Hell is a temporary holding place like the county jail, but the lake of fire is the permanent abode of all who rejected Christ. It is God's federal penitentiary for sinners. Believe me; the federal penitentiary and the lake of fire have little in common, as the former would be a paradise in comparison. In the past, on church visitation, I was able to visit a man who shared with me that he had spent 15 years in a maximum-security federal penitentiary. He knew and was known by mafia figure John Gotti and many other well-known gangsters, having himself been involved in organized crime. He confessed to me that the federal penitentiary was a horrible place and he was very thankful to get out. Fortunately, he heard the gospel in prison and trusted Christ as his savior, despite the jeers and mockery of many of his gangster friends. God's federal penitentiary, the lake of fire, will have no end, and there will be no possibility of pardon, parole, or escape. It is perpetual; final; eternal!

The sins of the Beast and False Prophet against God and humanity are so grievous that they are the only two humans who will be immediately judged before the final judgment one thousand years later. When Satan is cast into the lake of fire at the final judgment, along with his fallen angels and all unbelieving humanity, the Beast and False Prophet will have already been there for those thousand years.

The lake of fire will be a place of perpetual night and

darkness. The Bible states in Jude 1:13, *to whom is reserved the blackness of darkness for ever.* For those who refused God's light, they will see nothing, being in darkness continually. This is opposite of God and what Heaven will be like.

This then is the message which we have heard of him, and declare unto you, that God is light, and in him is no darkness at all (1John 1:5).

And the gates of it (heaven) shall not be shut at all by day: for there shall be no night there (Revelation 21:25).

And there shall be no night there; and they need no candle, neither light of the sun; for the Lord God giveth them light: and they shall reign for ever and ever (Revelation 22:5).

Heaven will be a place of basking in the glory of God with eternal brilliance. In stark contrast, the final abode of the Beast and his followers will be eternal night.

Part Three

The False Prophet

Chapter 15

The False Prophet

The last member of the Unholy Trinity is the man who is called another beast and the False Prophet. Most people will never catch on to what a slick deceiver he is. The triad of evil which I refer to as The Unholy Trinity will present such a positive image as heroes, that most people will be easily deceived. Concerning the many religious leaders today, the Bible says, *that, if it were possible, they shall deceive the very elect* (Matthew 24:24). Professing Christians by the thousands today are already following numerous false prophets without having a clue. When the disciples asked Jesus in Matthew 24:3, *what shall be the sign of thy coming, and of the end of the world?* His first response was, *Beware of false prophets, which come to you in sheep's clothing, but inwardly they are ravening wolves* (Matthew 7:15). Satan is a master deceiver and master of disguise, appearing to be an angel of light. The Beast will likewise be a master deceiver, seducing the world into believing he is the messiah and deserves their worship. The False Prophet will complete the deception appearing as a lamb though really a wolf in sheep's clothing. He will cause the whole world to worship the Beast by persuasion and coercion.

Despite his craftiness, he is surprisingly easy to identify, for those who are really seeking the truth. The advantage he has is that people look at spiritual things (i.e., God, the Bible, etc.) through the eyes (perspective) of man, rather than looking at men through the eyes (perspective) of God. To filter things from God's perspective, you must know the Lord personally as Savior and also have an intimate knowledge of the Bible. God felt this is so important he put a verse right in the middle of the Bible to clue us in. It is Psalms 118:8 and I call it God's Greatest Advice. It states, *It is better to trust in the LORD than to put confidence in man.* Notice something awesome: God put his name in the middle of the middle verse of the Bible, in a verse which reveals an enormous truth all by itself. (An important side note is that his name is not in the middle in most modern versions, but it is in the Authorized Version/King James Bible).

Many verses in the Bible must be taken in context and don't speak clearly by themselves. However, this verse can stand alone and be interpreted correctly by anyone who takes it at face value. Obviously, most people put more confidence in man, (priest, pastor, rabbi, other spiritual leaders, and even TV psychologists and other personalities), rather than God, through the Bible. Maybe the reason is that it is much easier to listen to people than to read and study the Bible for ourselves.

Let's set aside for a moment our indoctrination by man and examine the False Prophet from God's perspective, through the Bible. While there are many antichrists and false prophets, the Bible refers to two specific men who will be The Antichrist and The False Prophet. So, the False Prophet will be a singular man and leader.

And the beast was taken, and with him the false prophet that wrought miracles before him, with which he deceived them that had received the mark of the beast, and them that worshipped his image. These both were cast alive into a lake of fire burning with brimstone (Revelation 19:20).
And the devil that deceived them was cast into the lake

of fire and brimstone, where the beast and the false prophet are, and shall be tormented day and night for ever and ever (Revelation 20:10).

The False Prophet will also appear as a lamb, but speak as a dragon. As a lamb he will appear to represent Christendom, but in reality, he speaks lies like the devil.

And I beheld another beast coming up out of the earth; and he had two horns like a lamb, and he spake as a dragon. (Revelation 13:11)
Again Jesus said, *Beware of false prophets, which come to you in sheep's clothing* ('Christian' religious garb), *but inwardly they are ravening wolves.* (Matthew 7:15)

Another passage sheds more light, *Now the Spirit* (Holy Spirit) *speaketh expressly* (right to the point), *that in the latter times* (now) *some shall depart from the faith, giving heed to seducing spirits, and doctrines of devils; Speaking lies in hypocrisy; having their conscience seared with a hot iron; Forbidding to marry, and commanding to abstain from meats, which God hath created to be received with thanksgiving of them which believe and know the truth.* (1Timothy 4:1-3)

This passage is very revealing as it identifies three specific characteristics of the religion of the False Prophet: Hypocrisy, Celibacy and Abstaining from Meats. They speak about holiness, but live unholy. As a young person in the Catholic Church, I was told by the priest that cursing, smoking, and drinking alcoholic beverages were sins. Later I discovered that drinking, smoking, and cursing among priests was common. At my sister's wedding the priest used the word 'Holy' several times referring to God and our expected behavior in marriage and life. At the reception to follow, he along with his fellow priests were dancing, smoking, and drinking. According to a

138

survey conducted by the National Clergy Council on Alcoholism they estimate that at least 10% of the nation's 58,000 priests and 150,000 nuns were alcoholics. There are 148 alcohol intervention and counseling programs for priests with another 65 being formed according to a 1981 clergy survey.[1] Priests also practice celibacy, a vow not to marry. Years ago, a catholic friend and I were discussing the above scripture passage and I asked him if he knew any clergy that forbid to marry. He responded contrary to Psalms 118:8 when he said, "Yes, but priests are supposed to be celibate!" I then turned to 1 Timothy 3:1-5 where it says,

> *This is a true saying, if a man desire the office of a bishop, he desireth a good work. A bishop then must be blameless, the husband of one wife, vigilant, sober, of good behaviour, given to hospitality, apt to teach; Not given to wine, no striker, not greedy of filthy lucre; but patient, not a brawler, not covetous; One that ruleth well his own house, having his children in subjection with all gravity; (For if a man know not how to rule his own house, how shall he take care of the church of God?)*

My friend's face turned white as the truth sunk in and he realized he had been trusting a man who conflicted with what God clearly states in His Word, the Bible. What a shock I had when I first discovered that the Apostle Peter was married. *And when Jesus was come into Peter's house, he saw his wife's mother laid, and sick of a fever* (Matthew 8:14). What man in his right mind would have a mother-in-law without a wife? (Actually, I love my wife's mother-in-law.)

I also reminded him how we were forbidden to eat meat on Fridays as Catholics growing up. (I still hate fish sticks). At some point this rule was changed and now Catholics only abstain from meats on certain holy days.

The False Prophet also deceives people through miracles.

And he doeth great wonders, so that he maketh fire come down from heaven on the earth in the sight of men, And deceiveth them that dwell on the earth by the means of those miracles which he had power to do in the sight of the beast; saying to them that dwell on the earth, that they should make an image to the beast, which had the wound by a sword, and did live. And he had power to give life unto the image of the beast, that the image of the beast should both speak, and cause that as many as would not worship the image of the beast should be killed. (Revelation 13:13-15)

The miracles that he does may be supernatural or technological, but probably a combination of them both. Through existing satellites, it will likely be possible in the future to make 'fire' come down from heaven, whether like lightning or laser. Also, to make an image with the appearance of life is realistic in our day of holographic and computer-generated images. Aside from technology, Satan has the ability to do miracles within God's parameters. Satan's powers will be expanded greatly during this time, to serve God's purpose.

Even him, whose coming is after the working of Satan with all power and signs and lying wonders, And with all deceivableness of unrighteousness in them that perish; because they received not the love of the truth, that they might be saved. And for this cause God shall send them strong delusion, that they should believe a lie: That they all might be damned who believed not the truth, but had pleasure in unrighteousness. (2Thessalonians 2:9-12)

When the Bible says, *That they all might be damned who believed not the truth, but had pleasure in unrighteousness* (2 Thessalonians 2:12), the truth spoken of is that which concerns

Jesus Christ and the salvation he freely offers through his blood shed on the cross to pay for our sins. The truth is that there is no other way. Jesus himself said, *I am the way, the truth, and the life: no man cometh unto the Father, but by me* (John 14:6). In Acts 4:12 it is written concerning Jesus, *Neither is there salvation in any other: for there is none other name under heaven given among men, whereby we must be saved.* The ecumenical movement with their lie that there are many acceptable religions is in direct contrast to God and the Bible, as stated by Jesus himself. One of the ways the False Prophet will overcome what the Bible teaches is to supersede it with miracles. This is nothing new, because most people think all miracles come from God. It is reasonable to deduce that the False Prophet would be the head of some church or religion. Are there any churches known for miracles that would be consistent with Bible Prophecy?

If you do an internet search for Catholic miracles, you will quickly discover that there have been many miracles reported in Catholic churches and shrines over the centuries. They include Eucharistic miracles, where the host has turned into human flesh and blood. There are also many apparitions of the Virgin Mary, of which Our Lady of Lourdes appearing to St. Bernadette and Our Lady of Fatima are two of the most famous. There have been weeping statues of Mary in Akita, Japan; Chile; Chittagong, Bangladesh; Sacramento, California in 1995 and Cuenca, Ecuador in 2004. These are supernatural miracles and are only a few of many such reported. Per the article below, they are greatly increasing in frequency.

The Supernatural with a Purpose for Humanity!

In recent history, apparitions by the Blessed Virgin Mary have been reported in unprecedented numbers, forms, and places. Many people mock them. Others disregard them as anti-intellectual. Still others explain them through New Age ideas of spiritual intentions of huge groups of people showing up, at the same time, with the same created reality, all seeing the same thing. However, there are some apparitions that are neither easy to explain, nor easy to mock. The messages come true. What does it mean?[2]

Not only are these miracles consistent with what the Bible predicts, but they conflict with what the Bible teaches. One simple example is that most of the apparitions are of the virgin Mary. The Bible is very clear that after Mary gave birth to Jesus, she had normal marital relations with Joseph and gave birth to four additional sons and at least two daughters. Hence, she was not a perpetual virgin, as the Catholic Church refers to her. *While he yet talked to the people, behold, his mother and his brethren stood without, desiring to speak with him* (Matthew 12:46). The Jews spake of him, *Is not this the carpenter's son? is not his mother called Mary? and his brethren, James, and Joses, and Simon, and Judas? And his sisters, are they not all with us? Whence then hath this man all these things* (Matthew 13:55,56)?

These were Jesus' step brothers and sisters and confirm that Mary was no longer a virgin. That Satan can have his followers produce miracles is further confirmed in the Old Testament story of Moses confronting Pharaoh in Egypt. Moses had his brother Aaron throw down his rod before Pharaoh and it turned into a serpent. Pharaoh's magicians, who the Bible called sorcerers (witchcraft), were able to duplicate this miracle. They also were able to turn water to blood and supernaturally cause frogs to multiply in the land, as did Moses. After that however, they could not duplicate any more of the miracles God performed through Moses, and testified to Pharaoh, *This is the finger of God.* While Satan and his followers can definitely perform supernatural miracles, they can only do what God allows. Satan's ability to perform miracles through the Beast and False Prophet will cause many to believe a lie because their confidence will be in men, rather than the Lord, through the Bible.

In the next chapter we will give a brief history of religion to show where the Antichrist, the False Prophet, and their religion have their origins.

Chapter 16

The Mystery of Babylon Revealed

A Brief history of Religion

Let's go back to the beginning for a quick lesson in the history of Satan developing his network, which God ultimately refers to as Mystery Babylon. *And upon her forehead was a name written, MYSTERY, BABYLON THE GREAT, THE MOTHER OF HARLOTS AND ABOMINATIONS OF THE EARTH* (Revelation 17:5). This refers not to the physical Babylon with its splendid hanging gardens, but to a mysterious religious system whose roots spring from that city. It can appropriately be called the Scarlet Harlot and God reveals the mystery in the Bible as we follow history.

After the fall of man in the Garden of Eden, Satan was able to assume the dominion of Planet Earth, which God had given to Adam. As Adam's children were all born with a sin nature, sin soon became a dominant power in the lives and lifestyles of humanity, which Satan gladly manipulated. Though the gospel was well known and passed down verbally from Adam to his descendants, most of mankind chose to believe the appealing lies of the Devil over the truth of God just as Eve initially did. God at that time promised that he would send a Savior through the bloodline of the woman. In Satan's attempt to destroy the bloodline that the Savior/Messiah would come through, he persuaded many of his fallen angels (devils) to intermarry with human women.

The Bible explains: *That the sons of God (angels/dev-ils) saw the daughters of men that they were fair; and they took them wives of all which they chose.* (Genesis 6:2)

There were giants in the earth in those days; and also after that, when the sons of God came in unto the daughters of men, and they bare children to them, the same became mighty men which were of old, men of renown. And GOD saw that the wickedness of man was great in the earth, and that every imagination of the thoughts of his heart was only evil continually. (Genesis 6:4,5)

In order to preserve the human race, God destroyed the entire world with a flood, saving only Noah and his family. Why did God only save Noah? He and his family were likely the only ones alive at that time who were not corrupted and still had a living faith in the coming promised Messiah, the Lord Jesus Christ.

But Noah found grace in the eyes of the LORD. These are the generations of Noah: Noah was a just man and perfect, (born again/spiritually mature), in his generations, and Noah walked with God. (Genesis 6:8,9)
And Noah builded an altar unto the LORD; and took of every clean beast, and of every clean fowl, and offered burnt offerings on the altar. (Genesis 8:20) [This was a work proving his faith, as these sacrifices pictured the future sacrifice of Christ on the cross.]

It is important to know that according to Biblical genealogy, Adam was still alive when Noah's father Lamech was born. Lamech was 56 years old when Adam died. Noah had 6 living ancestors who could have known Adam. Adam passed down to all his ancestors the story of his fall in the Garden of

Eden and God's promise to send his Son as a sacrificial lamb. When the Bible says, *Noah found grace in the eyes of the LORD*, this is a reference to his belief in the coming Messiah, the only Lord, Jesus Christ. Abraham, the father of the Jews and Arabs, lived while Noah's son Shem was still alive. In the book of Genesis, it says of Abraham in Genesis 15:6, *And he believed in the LORD; and he counted it to him for righteousness.* One of the earliest men in the Bible, a man named Job, speaking of Christ, said *For I know that my redeemer liveth, and that he shall stand at the latter day upon the earth* (Job 19:25). Contrary to popular belief, many people in the Old Testament period knew about the coming Messiah.

One of Noah's sons, Ham had a grandson who Satan would use in his first attempt at a one world government and religion. His name was Nimrod and he rejected God and his plan of salvation, choosing instead the enticing promises of Satan. After the flood, animals, including dinosaurs, became wild and became a problem as their population grew. Nimrod became a popular hero in hunting and killing the dangerous beasts and later organizing cities with protective walls to keep the animals out.

The Bible states, *And Cush begat Nimrod: he began to be a mighty one in the earth. He was a mighty hunter before the LORD: wherefore it is said, Even as Nimrod the mighty hunter before the LORD. And the beginning of his kingdom was Babel, and Erech, and Accad, and Calneh, in the land of Shinar.* (Genesis 10:8-10)

When the Bible says Nimrod was a mighty hunter before the Lord, it has the connotation of him placing himself before the Lord in position and priority. In other words, Nimrod chose to be #1 and reject God's authority in his life, just as so many do today. The name Nimrod is synonymous with rebellion. Satan found in him a willing dupe to carry out his battle plan against God. The beginning of his kingdom was Babel, famous for its tower where God confused the language, creating the many languages we have today (up till then there was only one universal language). This simple act of God put a stop to Nimrod's plan to be world ruler as the people dispersed due to their sudden inability to communicate. The city was later known as Babylon and the area as Iraq. The tower was likely a ziggurat, a pagan temple used to worship false gods, and specifically the sun god. These temples have been found in many pagan civilizations, as those of the Aztecs and Incas. They were frequently associated with human sacrifice, prostitution, and other wicked practices. Despite the setback as world ruler, Nimrod, along with his beautiful and seductive wife, Semiramis, developed an idolatrous religion known generally as Baal worship. They developed a celibate priesthood who mystified the people with their secret rituals, while controlling the population through the requirement to confess their misdeeds to the priests to obtain forgiveness. The priests had tremendous power as they were privy to sensitive information about the individuals. This may have been the beginning of what we know today as blackmail. The priests could also ask leading questions to young girls and plant decadent thoughts in their minds. In this way many of the girls were seduced and many became vestal virgins, a respectable name for their service as temple prostitutes. The mystery Babylonian religion became so decadent and an affront to God that Nimrod's great uncle Shem, (Noah's son) killed him, cutting his body into pieces and sending them throughout the kingdom as a warning to his followers. Nimrod's wife Semiramis proclaimed that he had become the sun god. She later became pregnant through relations with one of the priests and then claimed her son Tammuz was supernaturally conceived and was Nimrod reborn as the sun god. Being familiar with the prophecy of God sending His own son as Messiah, Semiramis claimed its fulfillment in Tammuz, and declared herself as Queen of Heaven. Although the sun god was most often known as Baal & the Queen of Heaven as Ashtaroth, to the Greeks she was Aphrodite; to the Romans as

Venus; and in Ephesus as Diana.

> *And they forsook the LORD God of their fathers, which brought them out of the land of Egypt, and followed other gods, of the gods of the people that were round about them, and bowed themselves unto them, and provoked the LORD to anger. And they forsook the LORD, and served Baal and Ashtaroth. And the children of Israel did evil again in the sight of the LORD, and served Baalim, and Ashtaroth.* (Judges 2:12, 13, 10:6)

The Babylonian religion grew and was characterized by pictures of the mother and child under various names in many countries prior to the birth of Christ.

> *Image Search- Semiramis-Tammuz; Isis-Horus; Devaki-Crishna; Shingmoo

Scores of pictures of Mary and baby Jesus can be found at the Gallery of the Marian Library/International Marian Research Institute, Dayton, Ohio.[1]

This religion became in a sense the mother of all religions, evolving and mixing with each culture. The main obstacle to it was the prophecy of the coming Christ who would pay for the sins of mankind. The birth, life, death, and resurrection of Christ (gospel) were a major blow to this Babylon Mystery religion of Baal worship. After Christ's resurrection, the true church was turning the world upside down through the preaching of the gospel. Satan immediately raised up false prophets to bring in *damnable heresies* (2Peter 2:1), and to corrupt the scriptures even as they were being penned by the apostles (2Corinthians 2:17). Despite this, the church remained pure and powerful for three centuries after the resurrection of Jesus Christ. Despite severe persecutions from most of the Roman emperors, Christianity continued to abound while the Roman Empire declined. Then a major change in Satan's strategy occurred. With persecution causing the true church to flourish, he decided to give the world his own version of the Christian Church. He found the right man to pull off his coup in a Roman General named Constantine.

The decline of the Roman Empire was marked by several power struggles for the position of emperor, often with co-emperors, one for the east and one for the west. Upon the death of <u>Constantius Chlorus</u> in July of 306 A.D., his son Constantine I was proclaimed emperor by his father's troops. In the same year he was accepted as Caesar in the west by Galerius. In October of that year, Maxentius, the son of Maximian, was proclaimed emperor by the Roman Senate and Praetorian Guard. A power struggle ensued as Maxentius and his brother-in-law Constantine (who had married his sister for political expediency) both claimed to be emperor. The struggle ended at the battle of Milvian Bridge, where Constantine won a decisive victory. The events surrounding that victory remain a great controversy in Christianity. Legend has it that on the eve of that famous battle, Constantine saw a vision in the sky of a cross with the words, In this sign conquer. He then put crosses on the shields of all of his soldiers and upon his great victory declared that he was converted to Christianity. He stopped the severe persecutions of his predecessor Diocletian and ultimately took the title of Pontifex Maximus. [According to Wikipedia, the Pontifex Maximus (which literally means "Greatest Pontiff") was the high priest of the <u>Ancient Roman</u> <u>College of Pontiffs</u>. This was the most important position in the <u>polytheistic</u> <u>Roman religion</u>, which was Baal worship.] This put Constantine as head over the government of Rome and its religion. He was supreme Pontiff both politically and spiritually. He supposedly changed Rome instantaneously from pagan religion to Christianity. While the cessation of persecution was welcome to the church, Constantine's conversion to Christianity was suspect for the following reasons:

1. There is no account of him being confronted with the true Word of God', and the gospel, which are essential

to salvation. *So then faith cometh by hearing, and hearing by the word of God* (Romans 10:17).

2. His vision of a cross in the sky relates to the signs and lying wonders which will be true of the antichrist. *Even him, whose coming is after the working of Satan with all power and signs and lying wonders* (2Thessalonians 2:9).

3. History tells us that he continued in devotion to the pagan gods of Mars and Apollo, and simply changed the names of statues of the pagan gods to that of Peter and other apostles.

4. He took the title Pontifex Maximus, which was a pagan title and intermingled paganism and Christianity.

5. Long after his supposed conversion he killed, his son, his second wife, several others of his relatives, and some of his most intimate friends, in resentment of some personal offenses. This certainly is not characteristic of a true Christian.

6. He was known as a pragmatist who acted mostly out of political expediency.

Constantine stopping the persecution of the church was a mixed blessing. While it was a welcome relief to Christians, persecution was the very thing that caused the church to be pure and flourish. His favoritism of Christianity and wedding it to the state had the effect of causing confusion and weakness. The true Christians fled the state church and were later persecuted by it. Prior to this each church was individual and autonomous each having its own bishop or pastor. There was no head over the collective churches, except the Great Shepherd, the Lord Jesus Christ.

Constantine had a bishop named Eusebius produce 50 copies of the Bible for use in the Christian church. These Bibles were based on the corrupt manuscripts which were influenced by the writings and work of Origen from the school of Gnosticism is Alexandria, Egypt. While Origen and Eusebius are

considered early church fathers by some, they are both identified as Gnostics or Enlightened Ones, who mixed paganism
with Christianity and denied the deity of Jesus Christ.[2] This
was the beginning of the false ecclesiastical church which sup-
pressed the true Bible and true believers. This ultimately led
to the dark ages, where millions of Bibles and believers were
burnt at the stake by the ecclesiastical church headquartered in
Rome. Though there are references to this church and its practices throughout the scriptures, it is clearly and precisely identified in chapter 17 of Revelation. Many refer to her as the
Scarlet Harlot.

Chapter 17

The Scarlet Harlot

To the average person, I realize that this chapter may be hard to believe. When I first made this connection many years ago, I was in denial with a sick feeling in the pit of my stomach. The problem was not the clarity of the truth, but overcoming the years of indoctrination which had induced me to believe a false reality. I had grown up very devoted to this religion. It is very important as you read this chapter to let the facts speak for themselves and trust God's Word rather than the teaching of men.

In the previous chapter we considered the beginning and development of a religious system the Bible refers to as Mystery Babylon. It had it's beginning in the city and kingdom of Babylon, but has its fulfillment and finality in another city and another kingdom. Babylon in the present day is located in Iraq, in the center of what we know as the Arab or Muslim world. Mystery Babylon however will have its fulfillment in Europe in what historically has been the center of Christendom.

God revealed to the apostle John the picture and explanation of Mystery Babylon which he penned in Revelation, chapter 17. What he saw was pictured as a woman with such an appearance of wealth, beauty, and power that he *wondered with great admiration.* Six times in chapter 17 this entity is referred to as a *woman.* In verse one we find that this woman is referred to as a *whore* that sits on *many waters.* As one woman cannot sit upon many waters, we realize that John saw a personification of something which will be a religious institution covering the earth. She is identified first of all as a *whore.* In today's society, porn stars, who are truly harlots, have gained a measure of respectability. So have homosexuals, which refer to themselves as gay. However, God has never changed his mind about their immoral and perverted lifestyles.

He says,

Know ye not that the unrighteous shall not inherit the kingdom of God? Be not deceived: neither fornicators (sex outside of marriage), *nor idolaters, nor adulterers* (sex with someone else's spouse), *nor effeminate* (homosexuals), *nor abusers of themselves with mankind, Nor thieves, nor covetous, nor drunkards, nor revilers, nor extortioners, shall inherit the kingdom of God. And such were some of you: but ye are washed, but ye are sanctified, but ye are justified in the name of the Lord Jesus, and by the Spirit of our God.* (1Corinthians 6:9-11)

So, in calling this church a *whore*, God looks at it in very derogatory terms. The true church of Jesus Christ is identified as his *bride* in Ephesians 5:25 and 32 with a marriage in Revelation 19:7. The personification therefore is that this is a church who is not the Lord's, but rather an unfaithful whore. That she sits upon many waters indicates that this harlot church spans the globe. Consider eleven other characteristics of this false church which will help you identify it and its leaders, the Antichrist and False Prophet:

1. **It is referred to as a woman.** (Revelation 17:3-6) Do you know of any religion who refers to herself as Mother Church and is prominent in most countries?

2. **This church has secretive political alliances with foreign kings and governments.** *With whom the kings of the earth have committed fornication* (Revelation 17:2). The Vatican is the only entity on earth that is both church and state in one. It is a sovereign state with its own

government and ambassadors. It also is the Roman Catholic Church. The word Vatican comes from the Latin and means divining serpent. The crest of the Vatican is a dragon. This is significant as the Bible states in Revelation 12:9 *And the great dragon was cast out, that old serpent, called the Devil, and Satan, which deceiveth the whole world.* While the political alliances between the Catholic Church and governments are a matter of historical record, let me share some contemporary examples: During World War II, Hitler of Germany, Mussolini of Italy, and Franco of Spain had all signed Concordats with the Vatican, placing these governments and their peoples under the religious governance of the Vatican and the Pope.

Webster's 1828 dictionary gives the following definition and example of a Concordat: ["In the canon law, a compact, covenant, or agreement concerning some beneficiary matter, as a resignation, permutation, promotion and the like. In particular, an agreement made by a prince with the Pope relative to the collation of benefices; such as that between the emperor Frederic III., the German princes, and the Popes legate, A.D. 1448."] Pope John Paul II confirmed these alliances by a confession at the wailing wall in Jerusalem. "We are deeply saddened by the behavior of those who in the course of history have caused these children of yours to suffer, and asking your forgiveness we wish to commit ourselves to genuine brotherhood with the people of the Covenant." —Pope John Paul II (12 March 2000) from a note left by the Pope at the Western Wall in Jerusalem.

These agreements are normally done without much public notice. A case in point more pertinent to US citizens: During the Reagan Administration- President Reagan, George Bush, Casper Weinberger, and George Schultz were all working to sign a concordat with the Vatican. More details of this will be covered in the chapter on the Black Knights. While the concordat came to notice and was opposed, they were successful in getting Congress to repeal an 1867 law that forbid diplomatic relations with the Vatican. [That law was enacted in response to the Vatican's involvement in our civil war and the assassination of President Lincoln, which will be discussed in a later chapter in the Black Knights.] After this law was repealed, our government accepted Pio Laghi, as the Vatican's Pro-Nuncio (Ambassador) to the United States in March of 1984. He became a Cardinal in 1991 and was known as a close friend of the George H.W. Bush family being found frequently in his company during the Bush presidency. He was known also as the Pope's man in Washington. It is curious that the ACLU or similar groups never complained of this blatant violation of what they call the separation of church and state. Since that time the Pope has been given grand receptions when visiting our country as the head of the Roman Catholic Church, with very few voices raised in opposition. No other visiting dignitary has had a reception coming close to that of the Pope. Does the Pope really have much influence on the kings of the earth? You tell me.

---

*Image Search- Pope and: Yasser Arafat- PLO; King Abdullah of Saudi Arabia; Fidel Castro; President & Senator Clinton; King Juan Carlos of Spain; Nancy Pelosi; Nelson Mandela-S. Africa; Vladimir Putin- Russia; etc., etc.

A picture of Nancy Pelosi bowing and kissing the Popes ring is particularly disturbing, and those are only a few examples of many.

3. **The color scarlet/red.** In Revelation 17:3, John said, *and I saw a woman sit upon a scarlet coloured beast, full of names of blasphemy, having seven heads and ten horns.* The color scarlet/red is the prominent color of the College of Cardinals at the Vatican. It is also related to Communism. The European Union (Revived Roman Empire) is socialist in nature, which is really communism in a more

157

acceptable form. This church will ride (sit upon) the EU and the Antichrist for a period.

*Image search- College of cardinals (use advanced settings & color red)

4. **The *names of blasphemy*:** Holy Father, Bishop of Rome, Vicar of Jesus Christ, Successor of the Prince of the Apostles, Supreme Pontiff of the Universal Church, Patriarch of the West, Primate of Italy, Archbishop and Metropolitan of the Roman Province, Sovereign of the State of the Vatican City, Servant of the Servants of God, and Pontifex Maximus are a few of the Pope's official titles. The Apostles never used such titles and Jesus referred to himself simply as the *Son of God*, and *Son of man*. He also commanded us to not refer to anyone as father in a religious sense. *And call no man your father upon the earth: for one is your Father, which is in heaven* (Matthew 23:9). The chapter on the Scarlet Knights will further explain why these titles are so blasphemous.

5. **The Bible identifies the colors of this church.** *The woman was arrayed in purple and scarlet colour* (Revelation 17:4), which are the official colors of the Vatican.

*Image search-Scarlet and purple clergy

6. **Opulence:** *Decked with gold and precious stones and pearls* (Revelation 17:4). The cathedrals of the Catholic church are among the most lavish and ornate buildings in the world. St. Peter's Basilica is the largest church in the world and its opulence is staggering.

7. **The *Golden Cup*** is a major symbol of one particular religion: *having a golden cup in her hand full of abominations and filthiness of her fornication* (Revelation 17:4). In Roman Catholic teaching the golden cup (chalice) is said to contain the very body and blood of Jesus Christ, who the Bible says today is seated at the right hand of the Father.

(Ephesians 1:20; Colossians 3:1; Hebrews 1:3,13, 8:1, 10:12; 12:2) Roman Catholic teaching claims that the priests are able to call Jesus down from heaven during the consecration of the host to repeat the crucifixion. "The mass is the unbloody sacrifice of the body and blood of Christ. The mass is the same sacrifice as that of the cross." (Baltimore Catechism No.3, pg. 196). This means the father would have to endure seeing his Son crucified continually each time a priest says the mass. This is an abomination to God of the highest order. The Lord's supper was to be a remembrance, not a repetition.

The Bible says, *And every priest standeth daily ministering and offering oftentimes the same sacrifices, which can never take away sins: But this man, after he had offered one sacrifice for sins for ever, sat down on the right hand of God.* (Hebrews 10:11,12)
Babylon hath been a golden cup in the Lord's hand, that made all the earth drunken: the nations have drunken of her wine; therefore the nations are mad. (Jeremiah 51:7)

*Image search-Pope and golden cup

8. **Gross Immorality**: *Filthiness of her fornication* (Revelation 17:4). The year 2001 was marked by widespread sex scandals involving pedophile priests. Most of these priests were simply reshuffled to other areas rather than defrocked. In the book, The Priest, the Woman, and the Confessional, written by Charles Chiniquy, a former priest and friend of Abraham Lincoln, he exposes how priests use the confession booth to seduce women and children. He states that having heard the confessions of over 200 priests, all but 21 admitted to abusing the confessional. In the chapter on the Scarlet Knights, we will examine the history of immorality of the popes. It is truly staggering. Jesus himself said we would know false prophets by their *fruits* (deeds).

159

Beware of false prophets, which come to you in sheep's clothing, but inwardly they are ravening wolves. Ye shall know them by their fruits. Do men gather grapes of thorns, or figs of thistles? Even so every good tree bringeth forth good fruit; but a corrupt tree bringeth forth evil fruit. (Matthew 7:15-17)

9. **The name Mystery Babylon:** *And upon her forehead was a name written, MYSTERY, BABYLON THE GREAT, THE MOTHER OF HARLOTS AND ABOMINATIONS OF THE EARTH* (Revelation 17:5). In the preceding chapter we showed the history and development of this mystery religion. The Confraternity Edition Roman Catholic New Testament, (Pg. 337, 1963) claims that Rome is Babylon. Also, there are several prominent books that identify Mystery Babylon as having its fulfillment in the Roman Catholic Church.[1] They are listed in the Bibliography. The mystery part is not hard to figure out. The mysterious chanting, talking, and praying by priests in a language (Latin) unfamiliar to most people; smoke, candles, and incense; mystical rituals of transubstantiation; and elaborate and very complex doctrine understood only by the clergy, all lend themselves to an aura of mystery. A study of the book of Acts in the Bible reveals that these practices were foreign to the apostles and the early church. Many cults have been birthed by the mystery religion begun in Babylon, whose fulfillment is in the Mother Church located in Rome.

10. **Religious Persecution:** *And I saw the woman drunken with the blood of the saints, and with the blood of the martyrs of Jesus* (Revelation 17:6). The history of the Catholic Church is a history of persecuting people who they consider heretics. Dr. Alberto Rivera, former high-level Jesuit, estimates the number at over 68 million. The Spanish

160

Inquisition from 1478-1834 is perhaps the best-known period of persecution under the Roman Catholic Church. During this period millions were tortured and burnt at the stake, having been accused of heresy. Foxes Book of Martyrs gives many examples of the tortures and executions for which Mother Church was responsible. The masterminds behind the Inquisition eventually were the Jesuits, though it was carried out by the priests of the Dominican order. This was done under the Office of the Holy Inquisition, which is now called the Congregation for the Doctrine of the Faith (names have been changed to protect the guilty). This office was formerly headed by Cardinal Joseph Ratzinger, who became Pope Benedict XVI. Spilling the blood of the saints and martyrs is usually not done directly by the Roman Catholic Church, but rather through the governments which she controls. While the inquisition is the best-known example, the bloodletting occurred prior to the inquisition and continues today wherever it can happen without much notice. A case in point is the story of Prudencio Baltodano, a father, a farmer, and an evangelical preacher from Nicaragua. Sandinista soldiers tied him to a tree, struck him in the forehead with a rifle butt, stabbed him in the neck with a bayonet, slit his throat from ear to ear, and then cut off his ears. "See if your God will save you," they jeered as they left him for dead. God did save Prudencio Baltodano and he and his family were reunited in the U.S. He appeared several years ago on Jerry Falwell's Old Time Gospel Hour program. The communist Sandinista government was headed by Roman Catholic Daniel Ortega, who studied law at Managua's Jesuit-run Universidad Centro-Americana.

11. **The location of the church-Rome:** The Lord knew that it would be hard for people to believe that a church and leader so loved by the world could be the false church. For that reason, he made the Seventeenth Chapter of Revelation so clear that despite whatever the church's name at that

time, people who sincerely seek the truth would be able to recognize her characteristics. Despite her official colors and golden cup being so clear, God went the extra mile to identify this false church in a way that was unmistakable. He precisely shows her location in two very specific passages. *And here is the mind which hath wisdom. The seven heads are seven mountains, on which the woman sitteth* (Revelation 17:9). Rome, the location of the Vatican, is known as the city of seven hills. "It is within the city of Rome, called the city of seven hills, that the entire area of Vatican State proper is now confined."[2] Horace wrote of Rome, "The gods, who look with favour on the seven hills ..." Ovid added, "But Rome looks around on the whole globe from her seven mountains, the seat of empire and abode of the gods." Augustine wrote, "Babylon is a former Rome, and Rome is a later Babylon."[3] Then in Revelation 17:18, *And the woman which thou sawest is that great city, which reigneth over the kings of the earth.* While many could make a good case for Rome being the seat of world power today through the church, no one could deny that it was during the time of the Apostle John writing this passage. It is very important to understand that Rome was not the beginning of Mystery Babylon, but is its fulfillment in these days before the return of Christ.

Let me end this chapter on a very personal note. Growing up as a very devout Roman Catholic, and then later being born again, I had great difficulty accepting much of the information which God revealed to me. When I first came to the realization that the false religious system described in Revelation chapter 17 was the very church that I grew up in, I literally felt sick in the pit of my stomach. While I could not think of any other church or religion that fit the criteria in this chapter, I went into denial for a year, and tried not to think about it. The Lord brought a man across my path that had been studying to be a priest in Catholic seminary, but got saved through faith in Christ and never finished seminary. He confirmed to me that these shocking things about the Catholic Church were true. My heart goes out to the billion+ people, including many of my relatives, who have been so thoroughly indoctrinated into a belief that this is the true church, and the Pope stands in the place of Jesus Christ on earth. My prayer is that all who read this book would have their faith in Jesus Christ and his Word, the Bible, above the teachings of any church or man. If you cannot accept what the Bible clearly teaches here, you will really struggle with what you learn about the Scarlet and Black Knights.

Chapter 18

The Scarlet Knights

(The Men in Red)

T he color scarlet is bright red and is certainly prominent in referring to the harlot church described in Revelation, chapter 17. As we saw in the last chapter, red is also prominent in the priesthood of the Catholic Church. The College of Cardinals (red) is where Popes are elected out of and as the name cardinal implies, they are all dressed in red. These men in red, or scarlet knights of the Vatican have an interesting beginning and the men who were elected popes have a very interesting history, especially in recent days. To properly understand them, it is vital to first look at what God clearly says in the Bible about those He would choose for leadership in the church. This leadership is never referred to as priests in the New Testament. They are referred to as elders, pastors, or bishops, which all refer to a man who is called to oversee(bishop), or shepherd (pastor) a local autonomous church. A bishop does not oversee all pastors and churches in the New Testament; he is the pastor, one and the same. The Apostle Paul instructs Timothy in the qualifications for that office.

This is a true saying, If a man desire the office of a bishop, he desireth a good work. A bishop then must be blameless, the husband of one wife, vigilant, sober, of good behaviour, given to hospitality, apt to teach; Not given to wine, no striker, not greedy of filthy lucre; but patient, not a brawler, not covetous; One that ruleth well his own house, having his children in subjection with all gravity; (For if a man know not how to rule his own house, how shall he take care of the church of God?) Not a novice, lest being lifted up with pride he fall into the condemnation of the devil. Moreover he must have a good report of them which are without; lest he fall into reproach and the snare of the devil. (1 Timothy 3:1-7)

It is abundantly clear that a pastor/bishop should be married. The passage even explains why. *For if a man know not how to rule his own house, how shall he take care of the church of God* (1Timothy 3:5)? Why then would the Catholic Church *forbid to marry* (celibacy)? The historical answer is that this religious system is a continuation of the Mystery Babylon religion and their pagan, celibate priesthood. The Bible's answer is much more dramatic:

Now the Spirit speaketh expressly, that in the latter times some shall depart from the faith, giving heed to seducing spirits, and doctrines of devils; Speaking lies in hypocrisy; having their conscience seared with a hot iron; Forbidding to marry, and commanding to abstain from meats, which God hath created to be received with thanksgiving of them which believe and know the truth. (1Timothy 4:1-3)

Priests/bishops being forbidden to marry and abstaining from meat during lent, (or every Friday, as I was growing up as a Catholic) are/were two standards of The Church. It becomes very clear why as a child I was taught that only a priest could properly interpret the Bible, and why it has been forbidden to the common man for most of the Catholic Church's history. Catholics who do read the Bible for themselves are shocked when they find out that the Apostle Peter was married.

And when Jesus was come into Peter's house, he saw his wife's mother laid, and sick of a fever (Matthew 8:14; also Mark 1:30, Luke 4:38).

As becomes very obvious, a key qualification for the pastorate is to be a married man, *husband of one wife*. As celibates, none of the Scarlet Knights, (cardinals and popes), meet the first criteria of God to be bishops or pastors in the church. Let's examine the history of just a few of them to see how they fit the additional qualifications of being *blameless*, and of *good behavior*. As one studies the history of the popes, it becomes obvious that many of these men were known for immorality and greed, not holiness. For instance:

The period between 870 and 1050 are referred to by historians as the Midnight of the Dark Ages.[1] It was marked by bribery, corruption, immorality and bloodshed by the popes. Sergius III (904-911) obtained the office by murder. His reign became known as the Rule of the Harlots.[2] Through his mistress Marozia he fathered several illegitimate children. Her mother, Theodora, helped appoint the next pope, John X (914-928) who was her lover. Marozia smothered him to death to put her lover, Leo VI, into the papal chair. His reign only lasted a year from 928-929 as Marozia assassinated him when she learned he was in love with a woman more decadent than herself. Soon after, she placed her teenage son, John XI as pope. According to the Catholic Encyclopedia he was likely the natural son of Sergius III. In 955 Marozia placed her grandson, John XII into the Papal chair at the age of 18. He was so corrupt that a group of 50 Italian and German bishops convened in Rome to place him on trial and remove him from office. He was summoned in writing to defend himself against charges of: sacrilege, simony (buying the office with money), perjury, murder, adultery, and incest. His response was to refuse the summons, pronounce a sentence of excommunication on all, and seek bloody vengeance on the leaders. Cardinal-Deacon John had his right hand struck off. Bishop Otgar was scourged, and another of the leaders had his nose and ears cut off.[3]

Pope Boniface VII (984-985) overpowered his predecessor John XIV and thrust him into the dungeon of Sant' Angelo, where he died a few months later. Boniface maintained his position through bloodshed and the lavish distribution of stolen money. He was so hated by the populace that upon his violent and sudden death in July 985, his naked body was dragged through the streets and flung under the statue of Marcus Aurelius. Pope John XV (985-996) split the churches finances among his relatives. Benedict IX (1033-1045) was made pope at the age of 12 through a money bargain with the powerful families that ruled Rome. Evil among popes was not restricted to this period of 870-1050. While many popes committed murder, Pope Innocent III (1198-1216) shed more blood than all of his predecessors in instituting the first Inquisition.[4] It is estimated that up to a million heretics were killed and their property confiscated by Pope Innocent, who was certainly misnamed. Consider also Pope Boniface VIII (1294-1303) who issued the Unam Sanctum, which officially declared the Roman Catholic Church to be the only true church, outside of which no one can be saved. It stated: "We, therefore, assert, define and pronounce that it is necessary to salvation to believe that every human being is subject to the Pontiff of Rome." The Catholic Encyclopedia says of Boniface VIII, "Scarcely any possible crime was omitted-infidelity, heresy, simony, gross and unnatural immorality, idolatry, magic, etc." He stated that "to enjoy oneself and to lie carnally with women or with boys is no more a sin than rubbing one's hands together."[5]

Cardinal Bernardin: an angel of light

Former President Bill Clinton bestowed upon Cardinal Bernardin the Medal of Freedom; the highest honor available to American civilians. Clinton also praised Bernardin as a voice of moderation in the church. According to the November 1997 Washington Blade, a homosexual newspaper, the Cardinal himself had arranged for the Windy City Gay Chorus to sing at his wake at Holy Name Cathedral in Chicago (it did so behind a sign prominently displaying its name). Bernardin was a friend of Call to Action (CTA- A liberal group of Catholic lay people in opposition to traditional Catholic dogma) and allowed them to operate on Church property. He even went so far as to speak out against Bishop Bruskewitz of Lincoln, Nebraska, for excommunicating CTA members in his own diocese. In retrospect, it is apparent that Cardinal Bernardin sympathized or actively promoted the liberal/dissenting side on virtually every church issue. (i.e. all male priesthood, homosexuality, birth control, etc.)

Accusations of Satanism: An exposé by the lay group Roman Catholic Faithful

The allegations concerning Cardinal Bernardin's involvement in Satanism are taken from an exposé by Roman Catholic Faithful, (RCF).

Roman Catholic Faithful first heard of Agnes' story from a friend in 1996. This friend of mine had met Agnes a few years earlier when she came to him for advice. He never gave me her name or location but only made reference to her situation because it fit into a conversation we were having regarding the Archdiocese of Chicago. In 1998, when I first learned who Agnes was, I found that she had been on RCF's mailing list for some time. I also learned that a private investigator, as well as a lawyer from Chicago who had provided RCF with information, had met with Agnes a few years earlier in an attempt to help her find a way to bear witness to what had happened to her. This same investigator and lawyer provided RCF with information they had obtained regarding the alleged sexual activity of the priest who had abused Agnes many years earlier. That priest was the young Joseph Bernardin.

The allegations of Agnes

Over the past 12 years, in sworn deposition, in accounts to investigators, in affidavits submitted in support of others' cases, in direct statements to Bernardin, in phone calls and letters to Church officials, and in correspondence with Vatican officials (all of which RCF has examined), Agnes has testified to the following story:

In the fall of 1957, in Greenville, S.C., Fr. Joseph Bernardin raped 11-year-old Agnes as part of a satanic ritual that involved, among others, Bishop John Russell of Charleston. Brought to the event by an abusive father, Agnes "was able, at first, to resist Bishop Russell physically, out of the knowledge that God had made me good, not bad as I was being told I was" (her words). As a young child, she had been victimized by a sadist cousin, and her identity was based upon resisting bad things, which included Bernardin. Bernardin then showed kindness and approval of her resistance, in order to gain her trust and get her to relax, and then he raped her. He followed the rape with a perverted use of a host, in an attempt to make Agnes swallow the guilt of the event.

In the fall of 1992, Agnes passed a polygraph examination regarding these events. She also, in early 1990, told her story to Malachi Martin, who had been recommended to her as someone who could get her information to the Vatican, which Agnes knew had sole and immediate jurisdiction over such a case. Martin wrote a novel, Windswept House, with the premise that Agnes had given him: that the Catholic hierarchy's tolerance of heresy, liturgical abuse, clerical sexual misconduct, and clerical pedophilia had one overarching explanation at root, a network of Satanists whose smoke had ascended high in the church. Her story is greatly theatricalized in the novel, but the essential fact of ritual rape is there, as is the spiritual reality of Christ's presence in the victimized child. Thirty-four years later, Agnes went to visit Bishop Russell in a nursing home. In and out of lucidity, he agreed to testify against Bernardin if asked. He died without the opportunity to do so.[6]

The lawsuit of Steven Cook

A former seminarian from the Archdiocese of Cincinnati, Steven Cook, filed a $10 million lawsuit against Bernardin and Cincinnati priest Ellis Harsham. The suit accused Harsham, when he was a priest at St. Gregory seminary in Cincinnati in the mid-1970s, of numerous coercive sexual acts against him, and then delivering him to Bernardin, then archbishop of Cincinnati, for the same purposes.

Agnes later came to know Steve Cook, and submitted an affidavit in support of his suit. Before he died, Cook told Agnes he was writing a book to tell the truth about his abuse, and he gave a different account of his lawsuit retraction than the one publicly accepted.

Someone who knew Cook earlier than Agnes, is a former seminarian that RCF interviewed who admitted to a four-year sexual relationship with a Catholic bishop who now heads a western diocese. This man stated that he also had forced sexual contact with Cardinal Bernardin, and that, through Bernardin, he came to know Steven Cook. This individual, interviewed in November of 1998 by RCF, claims to have received a cash settlement. RCF confirmed, through an attorney, that this seminarian did indeed receive a cash settlement.

In June of 1998 RCF interviewed a Chicago businessman whose son was abused by a Chicago priest a few years earlier (1980's). In 1989 this Chicago businessman met with Cardinal Edouard Gagnon. He gave me the following account of his conversation with the Cardinal. He also directed me to Jason Berry's book LEAD US NOT INTO TEMPTATION for an account of his family's story. The Cardinal stated that the Holy See had received hundreds of letters regarding the pedophile problem in the U.S. and that it was beyond the control of the Holy See as the Church is in schism and the American bishops will not obey the Holy Father.[7]

As is obvious, Cardinal Bernardin was never excommunicated or even removed from office.

Pope John Paul I

Albino Luciani became Pope John Paul I on August 26, 1978 and died only 33 days into his Pontificate on September 28, 1978. While the official cause of death was ruled myocardial infarction (a heart attack) there is much speculation that it was caused by the use of the poisonous variety of digitalis, a plant which has both medicinal and toxic qualities. One half teaspoon would be enough to cause a fatal heart attack. It was said he intended to clean up the Vatican Bank scandal with dismissals and new appointments. The Vatican Bank, controlled by the Pope, involved illegal schemes and money laundering. Financial dealings were linked with the Masons, the Mafia, arms dealers, political kickbacks and monies funneled through the CIA to support Solidarity in Poland. He also intended to deliver a strong message about possibly terminating the Jesuits. He went to bed with a copy of his speech terminating the Jesuits and was found dead by his housekeeper the following morning. There was never an autopsy performed on him despite several mysterious circumstances surrounding his death.[8]

Pope John Paul II

The Scarlet Knight taking the place of Pope John Paul I was Karol Józef Wojtyla, becoming Pope John Paul II, the first ever Polish pope. According to Wikipedia, John Paul II was widely acclaimed as one of the most influential leaders of the twentieth century. In the website popejohnpaul.com he is said to be "The most revered human being on earth". This is quite a telling statement as the Lord Jesus Christ was despised and rejected of men and said that his followers could expect the same. *And ye shall be hated of all men for my name's sake* (Luke 21:17).

A catholic website www.patrickpollock.com states that Pope John Paul II committed over 100 heresies against Roman Catholic teaching. "If anyone holds to one single one of these (heresies) he is not a Catholic."[9] A few things done by Pope John Paul II that violate historical catholic teaching:

- Pope John Paul II allows his forehead to be marked by a Pagan Shiva priestess
- Pope John-Paul II preaches in a Lutheran church (Dec.11, 1983),
- takes part in Animist rites in the Sacred Forest in Togo (Aug. 8, 1985);
- has the sacred Tilac put on his forehead, a custom originating with priestesses of Shiva in Bombay (Feb. 2,1986);
- recited psalms with Jews while visiting the synagogue of Rome (April 13, 1986)
- invites Catholics and Jews to prepare together for the coming of the Messiah (June 24, 1986),
- engaged in dialogues with the high priests and witch doctors of Voodoo (Feb. 4 1993);
- invited representatives of all the main religions (about 130 came) to Assisi to pray for world peace (Oct. 27, 1986).

It seems that the view that one gets of the popes from the mainstream media is quite different from that of other sources which have carefully been censored from normal public view.

Pope Benedict XVI

Pope Benedict XVI, formerly Cardinal Joseph Ratzinger, served as Prefect of the Congregation for the Doctrine of the

Faith from November 1981 to April 2005. This office was formerly known as the Office of Inquisition. "As a tribunal, it judges heresy and all offenses leading to a suspicion of heresy. Its members are bound to the strictest secrecy, called the Secret of the Holy Office"[10] This is the same infamous entity responsible for the Inquisition of the dark ages where millions of Christians, Jews, and others were accused of heresy, interrogated by the cruelest tortures imaginable, and their property seized by the church. They were then executed by the secular governments in power who were subservient to the Pope fearing his enormous political power. In this way the Vatican claims no responsibility for their death. Though its name has been changed and it cannot operate as openly, the purpose has never changed. The man who formerly headed it was Cardinal Joseph Ratzinger, aka Pope Benedict XVI.

Consider some news items concerning him:

In October 1, 2006, the BBC aired a documentary in the UK entitled <u>Sex Crimes and the Vatican</u>, that implicated Pope Benedict XVI, as Cardinal Joseph Ratzinger, in the systematic cover-up of widespread child sex abuse allegations against Catholic priests. The Pope led a cover-up of child abuse by priests. The Pope played a leading role in a systematic cover-up of child sex abuse by Roman Catholic priests, according to a shocking documentary to be screened by the BBC tonight. In 2001, while he was a cardinal, he issued a secret Vatican edict to Catholic bishops all over the world, instructing them to put the Church's interests ahead of child safety. The document recommended that rather than reporting sexual abuse to the relevant legal authorities, bishops should encourage the victim, witnesses and perpetrator not to talk about it. And, to keep victims quiet, it threatened that if they repeat the allegations they would be excommunicated."[11]

Several years ago, he sent out an updated version of the notorious 1962 Vatican document Crimen Sollicitationis - Latin for The Crime of Solicitation - which laid down the Vatican's strict instructions on covering up sexual scandal. It was regarded as so secret that it came with instructions that bishops had to keep it locked in a safe at all times.

Benedict XVI Visits Mosque-A Gesture of Esteem at Istanbul Landmark

ISTANBUL, Turkey, NOV. 30, 2006 - Benedict XVI visited the Blue Mosque, the largest and most beautiful in Istanbul, as a public gesture of his esteem for Muslim faithful.

The Holy Father removed his shoes before entering the mosque, accompanied by the Grand Mufti and by the landmark's imam, Emanullah Hatiboglu. ... "It is a message of fraternity, in memory of this visit which I shall surely never forget," said Benedict XVI. He is the second Pope to enter a mosque's enclosure. John Paul II visited the Umayyad Mosque in Syria in May 2001.[12]

VATICAN CITY - A day after reaching out to other Christians and to Jews in his installation Mass, Pope Benedict XVI met Monday with members of the Muslim community, assuring them the church wanted to continue building "bridges of friendship" that he said could foster peace in the world. The Apostle Peter penned a whole chapter of the Bible warning about false prophets, not building bridges with them.

He begins, *But there were false prophets also among the people, even as there shall be false teachers among you, who privily shall bring in damnable heresies, even denying the Lord that bought them, and bring upon themselves swift destruction. And many shall follow their pernicious ways; by reason of whom the way of truth shall be evil spoken of.* (2Peter 2:1,2)

The Muslims not only consider Christianity as heresy, but have killed Christians throughout history as part of their credo. Peter never suggested building bridges with them, but rather preaching the gospel to them. How interesting that the man formerly in charge of protecting the church from heresy would give reverence to a religion in direct opposition to true

Christianity. What is his agenda? Is he building a bridge to a New World Order? Does any other religious leader have a following that even compares to that of the Pope?

Jesus speaking of his followers said, *Then shall they deliver you up to be afflicted, and shall kill you: and ye shall be hated of all nations for my name's sake* (Matthew 24:9).

In fact three more times Jesus said, *And ye shall be hated of all men for my name's sake* (Matthew 10:22; Mark 13:13; Luke 21:17).

Peter and most of the apostles were severely persecuted and suffered martyrs' deaths. Quite a contrast to this prophetic statement by the Lord Jesus Christ is the Pope, who is loved by most of the world.

Pawel Kopczynski/Reuters

Pope Benedict XVI, formerly a Nazi soldier, visited Auschwitz, walking through the infamous gate promising "Work Shall Set You Free." In contrast, Jesus said, *And ye shall know the truth, and the truth shall make you free* (John 8:32).

By IAN FISHER
Published: May 29, 2006
Auschwitz, Poland, May 28 — Pope Benedict XVI prayed on Sunday at the cells and crematories of the concentration camp complex here, on a visit he called "particularly difficult and troubling for a Christian, for a pope from Germany." "Words fail," said Benedict, born Joseph Ratzinger in Bavaria in 1927. The son of a policeman, he was inducted into the Hitler Youth and the German Army. "In the end, there can only be a dread silence, a silence that itself is a heartfelt cry to God." "Why, Lord, did you remain silent?" he said, his voice wobbling. "How could you tolerate this?" (Here is a former Nazi soldier accusing God for what Hitler and his Nazi soldiers did with full Vatican support.)

Pope Benedict XVI has marveled that a German Nazi like

himself could have been elected to lead the world's Catholics only 60 years after the horrors at Auschwitz. Pope Benedict XVI resigned his office on February 28, 2013, the first pope to ever resign, paving the way for the first Jesuit pope in history, Pope Francis.

There had been frequent power struggles between the popes and the Jesuits throughout history. As previously mentioned, Pope John Paul I died mysteriously after 33 days in office. He had planned to terminate the Jesuit order. The long power struggle ended on March 13, 2013 when Jorge Mario Bergoglio became Pope Francis, the first Jesuit pope in history.

Pope Francis

Pope Francis was born Jorge Mario Bergoglio on December 17, 1936 in Buenos Aires, Argentina, and as of December 2020 is 84 years old. He entered the Jesuit order in 1958 and became a full Jesuit on March 12, 1960. He became the Provincial Superior of the Jesuits in Argentina from 1973-1979, where he was the political rival of Argentine President Nestor Kirchner. He was then removed from his office by Peter Hans Kolvenbach, the Superior General of the Jesuits, often referred to as the Black Pope, (due to their black clothing). His removal was due to philosophical conflicts. Kolvenbach resigned and withdrew from his office on January 14, 2008, only the second ever to resign, as their appointment is for life. He was replaced by Adolfo Nicolas.[13] The unusual resignations of Kolvenbach and Pope Benedict paved the way for Pope Francis. He is known as a man of peace and humility, committed to social justice. He has told La Civilta Cattolica, a Jesuit periodical in Rome that the church should not speak out against abortion and homosexuality, but should be more welcoming. In June 2019 he declared a global climate emergency, which was taken up by our national media and several liberal politicians. [A side note is that global warming was changed to climate change, when the concept was disproven by many climatologists.] Pope Francis is against fossil fuels (gas & oil that runs our automobiles, planes and trains, and other industries). He also promotes the socialist/Marxist idea of wealth redistribution to alleviate poverty. These ideals have caused socialist countries like Cuba and Venezuela to greatly impoverish their citizens, while establishing a wealthy aristocratic ruling class who constantly talk of helping the poor and the working man. It is of note that Pope Francis' personal net worth is estimated at between $25-28 million dollars. This is aside from Vatican assets of over 15 billion dollars, which he controls. He is a vocal opponent of national sovereignty, right wing popularism, and our constitutional form of government. He aggressively supports globalism and the need for a one world church and government; i.e., the New World Order.

In an article reported in Fox News 10/21/2020, Pope Francis supports homosexuality. Pope Francis has voiced his support for same-sex civil unions for the first time as pontiff during an interview for the documentary film <u>Francesco</u>, which premiered at the Rome Film Festival on Wednesday. Francis has previously endorsed civil unions for gay couples as an alternative to same-sex marriages while serving as archbishop of Buenos Aires, but he never publicly voiced his support on the issue as pope until the interview. "Homosexual people have the right to be in a family," Francis said in the film. "They are children of God. What we have to have is a civil union law; that way they are legally covered." Pope Francis, who claims to speak ex cathedra for God is in direct conflict with what God says in Paul's letter to the church at Rome.

Because that, when they knew God, they glorified him not as God, neither were thankful; but became vain in their imaginations, and their foolish heart was darkened. Professing themselves to be wise, they became fools, And changed the glory of the uncorruptible God into an image made like to corruptible man, and to

birds, and fourfooted beasts, and creeping things.
Wherefore God also gave them up to uncleanness
through the lusts of their own hearts, to dishonour their
own bodies between themselves: Who changed the
truth of God into a lie, and worshipped and served the
creature more than the Creator, who is blessed for
ever. Amen. For this cause God gave them up unto vile
affections: for even their women did change the natural
use into that which is against nature: And likewise,
also the men, leaving the natural use of the woman,
burned in their lust one toward another; men with men
working that which is unseemly, and receiving in them-
selves that recompence of their error which was meet.
And even as they did not like to retain God in their
knowledge, God gave them over to a reprobate mind,
to do those things which are not convenient. (Romans
1:21-28)

Though this is very explicit, God also condemns sodomy,
(also called homosexuality and the gay lifestyle), in many other
scriptures. (Leviticus 18:22; 20:13; 1Kings 14:24; 15:12;
22:46; Deuteronomy 23:17) These are in addition to the well-
known story of God destroying the cities of Sodom and Go-
morrah in Genesis, chapter 19.

People can choose to believe what they are told in the
press, or they can look at the facts without the spin of the controlled media. Because someone talks like a Christian and
gives the appearance of being a Christian, does not mean they
are. Jesus himself sternly warned, *Beware of false prophets,*
which come to you in sheep's clothing, but inwardly they are
ravening wolves. Ye shall know them by their fruits (Matthew
7:15,16).

Could Pope Francis indeed be an antichrist instead of
Christ's representative on earth? Few people today would consider that possibility. However, until recent days, there was a
strong consensus among the leaders of most every major

denomination as to the identity of Antichrist. They were influenced more by the Bible and less by the media and books. Consider their perspective:

Martin Luther
(1483-1546) (Lutheran)
"We here are of the conviction that the papacy is the seat of the true and real Antichrist . . . personally I declare that I owe the Pope no other obedience than that to Antichrist." (Aug. 18. 1520 <u>The Prophetic Faith of Our Fathers</u>, Vol.2 pg. 121 by Froom.)

John Calvin
(1509-1564) (Presbyterian)
"Some persons think us too severe and censorious when we call the Roman pontiff Antichrist. But those who are of this opinion do not consider that they bring the same charge of presumption against Paul himself, after whom we speak and whose language we adopt. I shall briefly show that Paul's words in II Thess. 2 are not capable of any other interpretation than that which applies them to the Papacy." Taken from <u>Institutes</u> by John Calvin.

Cotton Mather
(1663-1728) (Congregational Theologian)
"The oracles of God foretold the rising of an Antichrist in the Christian Church; and in the Pope of Rome, all the characteristics of that Antichrist are so marvelously answered that if any who read the Scriptures do not see it, there is a marvelous blindness upon them." Taken from <u>The Fall of Babylon</u> by Cotton Mather in Froom's book <u>The Prophetic Faith of Our Fathers</u>, Vol. 3, pg.113.

John Knox

(1505-1572) (Scotch Presbyterian)

Knox wrote to abolish "that tyranny which the pope himself has for so many ages exercised over the church" and that the pope should be recognized as "the very antichrist, and son of perdition, of whom Paul speaks." Taken from The Zurich Letters, pg. 199 by John Knox.

Thomas Cranmer

(1489-1556) (Anglican)

"Whereof it followeth Rome to be the seat of antichrist, and the pope to be very antichrist himself, I could prove the same by many other scriptures, old writers, and strong reasons." (Referring to prophecies in Revelation and Daniel.) Taken from Works by Cranmer, Vol 1, pp. 6-7.

John Wesley

(1703-1791) (Methodist)

Speaking of the Papacy he said, "He is in an emphatical sense, the Man of Sin, as he increases all manner of sin above measure. And he is, too, properly styled the Son of Perdition, as he has caused the death of numberless multitudes, both of his opposers and followers. He it is … that exalteth himself above all that is called God, or that is worshipped, ... claiming the highest power, and highest honour, ... claiming the prerogatives which belong to God alone." Taken from Antichrist and His Ten Kingdoms by John Wesley, pg. 110

Roger Williams

(1803-1683) (First Baptist Pastor in America)

He spoke of the Pope as "the pretended Vicar of Christ on earth, who sits as God over the Temple of God, exalting himself not only above all that is called God, but over the souls and consciences of all his vassals, yea over the Spirit of Christ, over the Holy Spirit, yea, and God himself, ... speaking against the God of heaven, thinking to change times, and laws; but he is the son of perdition (II Thess. 2)" Taken from The Prophetic Faith of Our Fathers, Vol. 3, pg. 52., by Froom.

C. H. Spurgeon
(1834-1892) (Baptist Preacher from England known as "Prince of Preachers")
"It is the bounden duty of every Christian to pray against Antichrist, and as to what Antichrist is no sane man ought to raise a question. If it be not the Popery in the Church of Rome there is nothing in the world that can be called by that name. It wounds Christ, robs Christ of His glory, puts sacramental efficacy in the place of His atonement, and lifts a piece of bread in the place of the Saviour. If we pray against it, because it is against Him, we shall love the persons though we hate their errors; we shall love their souls, though we loathe and detest their dogmas."

The Westminster Confession
"There is no other head of the Church but the Lord Jesus Christ (Colossians 1:18). Nor can the Pope of Rome, in any sense, be head thereof; but is that Antichrist, that man of sin, and son of perdition, that exalts himself, in the Church, against Christ and all that is called God." (Matt. 23:8) Chapter 25, Section VI.

There are other more contemporary figures like Charles Finney and D. L. Moody who agreed, but the above mentioned clear up much confusion in the matter of who the Antichrist will be. Though the history of the Scarlet Knights has been carefully reconstructed and kept from public view, those who truly desire and seek the truth will

182

find it. While it is very difficult to know what goes on behind closed doors concerning the Popes and Cardinals, God has allowed enough information to leak out so that their fruits are evident. Unfortunately, what I have shared is only the very small tip of a very large iceberg.

Chapter 19

The Black Pope

The most mysterious man in the world is the Black Pope. The most obscure man in the world is the Black Pope. Probably the most powerful and dangerous man in the entire world is the Black Pope. Who is the Black Pope? Should we first ask, what is the Black Pope? The Black Pope is the General Superior of the Society of Jesus, usually called the Jesuit Order. Simply stated the Black Pope is the Jesuit General. His historical purpose is to cause every person on planet earth to bow in submission to the Pope. In this he perfectly fits the biblical role of the False Prophet who will cause everyone to bow to the Antichrist. He is likely the most feared man in the world among the rich and powerful due to his vast network of power, influence and ability to eliminate the opposition. To understand the Black Pope, we need to go back to the first one and the beginning of the Society of Jesus.

One of the worst times in the history of the world was known as the Dark Ages. It was a time of darkness; spiritually, economically, politically, morally and physically. It was marked by the dominance of the Roman Catholic Church and a great repression of the Bible and distortion of the pure gospel of Christ. There was widespread ignorance of the Scriptures, education, and science. This led to great outbreaks of disease, and loss of liberty. The average life expectancy during this time was only about thirty years of age. During this time of religious oppression, God continually raised up men to preach the truth as they came in contact with the Word of God, the Bible. Some of these men were Savonarola, John Huss, John Wycliffe, William Tyndale, and Martin Luther, among many others. These were used by God to bring a reformation; a return to the Bible and its truth about Jesus Christ alone being the way of salvation.

On October 31, 1517A.D. Martin Luther nailed a document to the church door at Wittenberg, Germany. This document was known as his Ninety-Five Theses and outlined the errors and abuses of the Catholic Church and its leaders. Most of these dealt with the selling of indulgences to get dead relatives out of purgatory and selling papal pardons for forgiveness of sins, though other abuses, like the buying of religious offices (simony), and immorality were also listed. This event was a major factor in turning many people to the Bible and from the Catholic Church. This was known as the Reformation or rise of Protestantism, where people protested the beliefs and conduct of the Papacy and Roman Catholic Church. The Catholic Church's response was the dreaded Dominican order and the cruel Inquisition, where millions were tortured and executed as heretics. Instead of stopping the rise of the gospel, it advanced it, as it did during the persecutions of the early church under the Caesars. Satan however, had another ace up his sleeve; enter Ignatius of Loyola.

In 1491, a boy was born to a devout Roman Catholic family in the castle of Loyola, in Guipuzcoa, Spain. He was named Ignacio López de Loyola. He later came to be known as Ignatius of Loyola, and made his career in the military. During the battle at Pamplona on May 20, 1521 he was seriously wounded when a French cannonball shattered his leg. He endured the horror of several surgeries without anesthesia and then went through a long and painful recovery that left him with a lifelong limp. During this time of recovery, he was greatly influenced by catholic writers and had visions of Mary and baby Jesus, which were consistent with the Babylonian Mystery religion as previously noted. He became an ascetic, inflicting severe discipline upon himself to obtain Christ. Instead of accepting Christ in simple faith through the Word of God, *So then faith cometh by hearing, and hearing by the word of God* (Romans 10:17), he devised his own Spiritual Exercises, to reach a state of enlightenment. This enlightenment was the same as the Gnostics achieved, initially originating in Babylon. There were several groups practicing this state of enlightenment called Illuminism. While he professed to seek the Lord Jesus Christ in his own way, he actually found Lucifer, whose name means the light bearer. The Bible solemnly warns in two places, *There is a way which seemeth right unto a man, but the end thereof are the ways of death* (Proverbs 14:12 & 16:25). Ignatius was deceived by the *angel of light* through his association with the Illuminati, also called the Los Alumbrados, or The Illumined Ones. This Illuminism and its method of seeking light is common to witchcraft and Freemasonry, and the Jesuits, though these groups are supposedly at odds with each other.

In 1537 Ignatius founded the Society of Jesus, known as the Jesuits, to fight the Protestant Reformation, and bring every human on earth to submit to the authority of the Pope as Christ's Vicar on Earth. Due to his strange activities, which seemed occult even to the Vatican, Ignatius was accused of heresy and brought before the inquisition by the Dominicans. While few ever survived the inquisition tribunal, Ignatius requested an audience with the Pope, and was granted it due to his acquaintance with kings and noblemen. He convinced the Pope that the purpose of the Society of Jesus was to be a military priesthood, totally dedicated to the Pope, with the ultimate goal of bringing the whole world under his temporal power. The Pope bought the idea and in 1541 the Pope officially sanctioned the Jesuit order with Ignatius of Loyola becoming the first Jesuit General. The Jesuit General is known as the Black Pope due to his black garments. In developing the Jesuit order Loyola developed a set of rules known as The Spiritual Exercises.

The following are the Spiritual Exercises of Loyola, which sound very spiritual. God warns us to *try the spirits*, because much that is religious or spiritual is not of God, but from the angel of light, Satan. I have added commentary in brackets to the first few rules so that we can examine his Spiritual Exercises in light of God's Word, the Bible.

[Many of the opinions of Ignatius Loyola, founder of the Jesuit Order, are in this document setting out rules for the order and for the Christian life. Note, as you read, what issues brought up by the Protestant Reformation he is protesting or countering.]

Medieval Sourcebook: St. Ignatius Loyola: Spiritual Exercises

"TO HAVE THE TRUE SENTIMENT WHICH WE OUGHT TO HAVE IN THE CHURCH MILITANT"

Let the following Rules be observed:

First Rule. The first: All judgment laid aside, we ought to have our mind ready and prompt to obey, in all, the true Spouse of Christ our Lord, which is our holy Mother the Church Hierarchical.
[Judgment laid aside is blind obedience, which the Bible never sanctions. Instead, it warns us to *try the spirits, Beloved, believe not every spirit, but try the spirits whether they are of God: because many false prophets are gone out into the world* (1 John 4:1). Holy Mother the Church Hierarchical relates specifically to the leadership of the Roman Catholic Church, which is clearly identified in Revelation 17 as the harlot church.]

Second Rule. The second: To praise confession to a Priest, and the reception of the most Holy Sacrament of the Altar once in the year, and much more each month, and much better from week to week, with the conditions required and due.
[The Bible nowhere tells us to confess to a priest or identifies sacraments, but instead tells us, *For there is one God, and one mediator between God and men, the*

man Christ Jesus (1 Timothy 2:5). The Bible tells us in 1 John 1:9, *If we confess our sins, he is faithful and just to forgive us our sins, and to cleanse us from all unrighteousness.* This confession is to God, not our fellow man or a priest.]

Third Rule. The third: To praise the hearing of Mass often, likewise hymns, psalms, and long prayers, in the church and out of it; likewise, the hours set at the time fixed for each Divine Office and for all prayer and all Canonical Hours.

[According to Catholic doctrine, the Mass is Christ offering himself as a sacrifice to the Father over and over again as he did on the cross (pgs. 45,46 Pocket Catechism, St. Joseph Edition, 1973). This is blasphemous to the Father as the Bible states, *So Christ was once offered to bear the sins of many* (Hebrews 9:28). *But this man, after he had offered one sacrifice for sins for ever, sat down on the right hand of God; For by one offering he hath perfected for ever them that are sanctified* (Hebrews 10:12,14). The last thing Jesus said on the cross before dying was, *It is finished.* To repeat that horrible event over and over is a gross abomination to God the Father.]

Fourth Rule. The fourth: To praise much Religious Orders, virginity and continence, and not so much marriage as any of these.

[As has been previously shown, the requirement to be a bishop, (religious orders) is marriage, not celibacy. He is advocating the opposite of the Bible. (1Timothy 3:2, 4:1-3)]

Fifth Rule. The fifth: To praise vows of Religion, of obedience, of poverty, of chastity and of other perfections of supererogation. And it is to be noted that as the vow is about the things which approach to Evangelical perfection, a vow ought not to be made in the things which withdraw from it, such as to be a merchant, or to be married, etc.

[Obedience and Chastity should be the norm for the Christian life, not a vow. A vow of poverty is contrary to many scriptures: *Beloved, I wish above all things that thou mayest prosper and be in health, even as thy soul prospereth* (3 John 1:2). *Poverty and shame shall be to him that refuseth instruction* (Proverbs 13:18). *For ye know the grace of our Lord Jesus Christ, that, though he was rich, yet for your sakes he became poor, that ye through his poverty might be rich* (2 Corinthians 8:9).]

Sixth Rule. To praise relics of the Saints, giving veneration to them and praying to the Saints; and to praise Stations, pilgrimages, Indulgences, pardons, Cruzadas, and candles lighted in the churches.

[This conflicts with the first and greatest commandment, *Thou shalt have no other gods before me* (Exodus 20:3), as it is idolatry, and the second and most detailed commandment, *Thou shalt not make unto thee any graven image, or any likeness of any thing that is in heaven above, or that is in the earth beneath, or that is in the water under the earth: Thou shalt not bow down thyself to them, nor serve them: for I the LORD thy God am a jealous God, visiting the iniquity of the fathers upon the children unto the third and fourth generation of them that hate me* (Exodus 20:4). This commandment has been eliminated by the Catholic church, and the 10th commandments split into two. Read Exodus 20: 3-17, where they are listed. The activities he commands to praise are great examples of the mystery in Mystery Babylon]

Seventh Rule. To praise Constitutions about fasts and abstinence, as of Lent, Ember Days, Vigils, Friday and Saturday; likewise, penances, not only interior, but also exterior.

*I hate, I despise your feast days, and I will not smell in your solemn assemblies (*Amos 5:21*). Bring no more vain oblations; incense is an abomination unto me; the new moons and sabbaths, the calling of assemblies, I cannot away with; it is iniquity, even the solemn meeting. Your new moons and your appointed feasts my soul hateth: they are a trouble unto me; I am weary to bear them.* (Isaiah 1:13-14)

Eighth Rule. To praise the ornaments and the buildings of churches; likewise, images, and to venerate them according to what they represent. [same as sixth rule]

Ninth Rule. Finally, to praise all precepts of the Church, keeping the mind prompt to find reasons in their defense and in no manner against them.
[The precepts he refers to are traditions of the Catholic Church, not the Bible. *Making the word of God of none effect through your tradition, which ye have delivered: and many such like things do ye* (Mark 7:13).]

Tenth Rule. We ought to be more prompt to find good and praise as well the Constitutions and recommendations as the ways of our Superiors. Because, although some are not or have not been such, to speak against them, whether preaching in public or discoursing before the common people, would rather give rise to fault-finding and scandal than profit; and so the people would be incensed against their Superiors, whether temporal or spiritual. So that, as it does harm to speak evil to the common people of Superiors in their absence, so it can make profit to speak of the evil ways to the persons themselves who can remedy them.
[While it is wrong to be a backbiter or critical of leadership without cause, we are to stand against error,

especially by church leaders as the Apostle Paul did to the Apostle Peter in Galatians 2:11, *But when Peter was come to Antioch, I withstood him to the face, because he was to be blamed.*]

Eleventh Rule. To praise positive and scholastic learning. Because, as it is more proper to the Positive Doctors, as St. Jerome, St. Augustine and St. Gregory, etc., to move the heart to love and serve God our Lord in everything; so, it is more proper to the Scholastics, as St. Thomas, St. Bonaventure, and to the Master of the Sentences, etc., to define or explain for our times the things necessary for eternal salvation; and to combat and explain better all errors and all fallacies. For the Scholastic Doctors, as they are more modern, not only help themselves with the true understanding of the Sacred Scripture and of the Positive and holy Doctors, but also, they being enlightened and clarified by the Divine virtue, help themselves by the Councils, Canons and Constitutions of our holy Mother the Church.

[The above men, councils and church have confused the things necessary for salvation. When the Philippian jailer asked Paul and Silas, *Sirs, what must I do to be saved? They said, Believe on the Lord Jesus Christ, and thou shalt be saved, and thy house* (Acts 16:30,31). A curse is on anyone who brings any other gospel and plan of salvation. *But though we, or an angel from heaven, preach any other gospel unto you than that which we have preached unto you, let him be accursed* (Galatians 1:8).]

Twelfth Rule. We ought to be on our guard in making comparison of those of us who are alive to the blessed passed away, because error is committed not a little in this; that is to say, in saying, this one knows more than St. Augustine; he is another, or greater than, St. Francis; he is another St. Paul in goodness, holiness, etc.

Thirteenth Rule. To be right in everything, we ought always to hold that the white which I see, is black, if the Hierarchical Church so decides it, believing that between Christ our Lord, the Bridegroom, and the Church, His Bride, there is the same Spirit which governs and directs us for the salvation of our souls. Because by the same Spirit and our Lord Who gave the ten Commandments, our holy Mother the Church is directed and governed.

Fourteenth Rule. Although there is much truth in the assertion that no one can save himself without being predestined and without having faith and grace; we must be very cautious in the manner of speaking and communicating with others about all these things.

Fifteenth Rule. We ought not, by way of custom, to speak much of predestination; but if in some way and at sometimes one speaks, let him so speak that the common people may not come into any error, as sometimes happens, saying: Whether I have to be saved or condemned is already determined, and no other thing can now be, through my doing well or ill; and with this, growing lazy, they become negligent in the works which lead to the salvation and the spiritual profit of their souls.

Sixteenth Rule. In the same way, we must be on our guard that by talking much and with much insistence of faith, without any distinction and explanation, occasion be not given to the people to be lazy and slothful in works, whether before faith is formed in charity or after.

Seventeenth Rule. Likewise, we ought not to speak so much with insistence on grace that the poison of discarding liberty be engendered. So that of faith and grace one can speak as much as is possible with the

Divine help for the greater praise of His Divine Majesty, but not in such way, nor in such manners, especially in our so dangerous times, that works and free will receive any harm, or be held for nothing.

Eighteenth Rule. Although serving God our Lord much out of pure love is to be esteemed above all; we ought to praise much the fear of His Divine Majesty, because not only filial fear is a thing pious and most holy, but even servile fear -- when the man reaches nothing else better or more useful -- helps much to get out of mortal sin. And when he is out, he easily comes to filial fear, which is all acceptable and grateful to God our Lord: as being at one with the Divine Love.[1]

The problem with the Spiritual Exercises is that they are not in harmony with God's Word. When any man tries to reach God on man's terms rather than God's clear commandments, it is an affront to God. Throughout the Bible nothing is made clearer than that Jesus Christ is the *way, the truth and the life,* and that *no man can come to the Father except through him* (John 14:6).

> *And this is the record, that God hath given to us eternal life, and this life is in his Son. He that hath the Son hath life; and he that hath not the Son of God hath not life. These things have I written unto you that believe on the name of the Son of God; that ye may know that ye have eternal life, and that ye may believe on the name of the Son of God.* (1John 5:11-13)
> *Verily, verily, I say unto you, He that entereth not by the door into the sheepfold, but climbeth up some other way, the same is a thief and a robber.* (John 10:1) *Then said Jesus unto them again, Verily, verily, I say unto you, I am the door of the sheep. All that ever came before me are thieves and robbers: but the sheep did not*

194

hear them. I am the door: by me if any man enter in, he shall be saved, and shall go in and out, and find pasture. (John 10:7-9)

It is obvious from the Bible and Jesus' own words that this excludes Mary, the saints, or any church.

With the Spiritual Exercises as his foundation, Ignatius utilized the following: 1. Philosophy 2. Metaphysics 3. Logic 4. Psychoanalysis 5. Psychology 6. Hypnosis 7. Telepathy 8. Parapsychology (scientific witchcraft) 9. Psychiatry and 10. Psychotherapy.[2] These are now called behavioral sciences, but are incompatible with the principles taught in the Bible.

While Ignatius emphasized the spiritual and talked about devotion to Jesus, his spirituality was occult. He demanded and trained his followers to submit to blind obedience to the Jesuit General. One famous Jesuit saying is to believe that black is white, and white is black, if thus spoken by a superior. This blind obedience without trying the spirits led to the one of the foundational principles practiced by the Jesuits: the end justifies the means. Another way of explaining it is that anything goes, or no holds barred, when done for the glory of God. While this may seem a contradiction in terms for most people, (and it is), it is standard operating procedure for the Jesuits. Lying, cheating, stealing, and even murder is acceptable when done in submission to a superior for the Church and Christ. While this may seem hard to swallow for the average person who may consider the Catholic clergy to be holy men, the reality of this truth will become obvious in the next chapter discussing the Black Knights. Again, Jesus warned of ministers in sheep's clothing who were ravening wolves.

The current Black Pope is Adolfo Nicolas, the 30th Superior General of the Jesuits. He was elected on January 19, 2008, when Count Peter-Hans Kolvenbach strangely retired. Normally the Black Pope serves for life. In an article concerning the new Jesuit General, journalist Jeff Israely makes the following statement: "The Jesuits eventually became the shock troops of the Church as it fought the Reformation, terrorizing Protestant regimes from England to the Netherlands to Sweden."[3]   My earlier statement about the Jesuit General being the most feared man in the world will be more clearly understood in the next chapter on The Black Knights. One example, however, will illustrate the reason why so many fear the Black Pope. It regards the circumstances surrounding the assassination attempt on Pope John Paul II.

"Just 3 weeks prior to the assassination attempt, Pope John Paul II had a meeting with 6 of the most powerful cardinals in the Vatican. The topic: the forced resignation of the Jesuit General Pedro Arrupe. On May 13, 1981, within three weeks of that private papal conference (to fire Arrupe), John Paul II was struck by two bullets from the Browning semiautomatic pistol of paid hitman Mehmet Ali Agca. At the height of the Pontiff's crisis, on May 28, Cardinal Wyszynski of Warsaw mysteriously died. Wyszynski was John Paul's closest friend, and was very influential in his ascent to Pope."[4]

The best way to understand the Black Pope and his role as the False Prophet, is to look at his work accomplished through his Men in Black, the Jesuits.

Chapter 20

The Black Knights

(Men in Black)

In a general sense the color black has often been associated with darkness, death, and evil. In the older movies the good guys wore white and bad guys wore black. In the church of Satan, the color black is prominent as are familiar terms like Black Mass and Black Sabbath. Viewing pictures of former Satanic High Priest Anton LaVey, or participants in a Black Mass, they are noticeably dressed in black. Often people involved in the occult have a tendency to dress in black. In a general sense the color white is often associated with light, life, good, and God. Wedding dresses are traditionally white, depicting purity. Angels are clothed in white.

*Please understand I am making a generalization. Wearing a black suit or shirt obviously does not make one evil, and wearing white does not make one good. But there is a reason for this association with color. It is rooted in the Bible. In Job 3:5 the Bible says, *Let darkness and the shadow of death stain it; let a cloud dwell upon it; let the blackness of the day terrify it.* In Jude 1:13 speaking of final judgment, it states, *to whom is reserved the blackness of darkness forever.* Conversely the Bible usually associates white and light with God. *This then is the message which we have heard of him, and declare unto you, that God is light, and in him is no darkness at all* (1 John 1:5). *Many shall be purified, and made white, and tried; but the wicked shall do wickedly: and none of the wicked shall understand; but the wise shall* understand (Daniel 12:10). Speaking

198

of the angel at the garden tomb, after Christ arose: *His countenance was like lightning, and his raiment white as* snow (Matthew 28:3). Speaking of Christ at the transfiguration, *And his raiment became shining, exceeding white as snow* (Mark 9:3). When Christians return at the battle of Armageddon, we will be clothed in white; *And the armies which were in heaven followed him upon white horses, clothed in fine linen, white and clean* (Revelation 19:14). Nowhere in the Bible will you find the Saints/Believers dressed in black. There is a good basis for identifying white and black as generally representing good and evil. It is interesting that Hollywood is starting to identify Men in Black as the good guys, the heroes, thereby departing from the historical precedent. A very important point is that this has nothing to do with skin color, which is only a matter of pigment percentage. Some of the greatest preachers have been black men and some of the most wicked criminals and leaders have been white folks.

When I use the term Black Knights, it conjures up the idea of a group bent on doing evil. There is such a group operating today and the term Black Knights is a very fitting name for them because their clothing is prominently black. They are Men in Black in their dress and in their deeds behind the scenes. These men have an influence on our world, our country, and you personally that will astound you. While their influence is major, their footprints are almost imperceptible. Their work is done primarily undercover with an obscure stealth. They are known to most as the Jesuits, and officially as the Society of Jesus. They are the Intelligencia and military arm of the Roman Catholic Church. Outwardly they present a very good image of good works and humanitarianism. However, their activities of espionage and political intrigue in the name of Christ would make the best James Bond novel seem bland in comparison. Even growing up as a Roman Catholic, I seldom heard much about the Jesuits, but the one word usually used to describe them was brilliant. Let's discover the source of their brilliance, their founder, their activities, and the extent to which they influence your life.

The Jesuits operated differently than other orders within the Catholic Church. Unlike the Dominicans primary use of terror and force during the Counter Reformation, the Jesuit mode of operation was to infiltrate governments, churches and other important institutions, including schools and universities. They were to be the teachers and mentors to kings, parliamentarians, and people in positions of power. [A contemporary example is the tutelage of former President Bill Clinton by famous Jesuit Professor Carroll Quigley at Jesuit Georgetown University.] They would gain control of economies through placing their agents into positions of influence. To accomplish these ends they would use sex, blackmail, bribery, and when necessary, opposition would be eliminated through scandals or ultimately assassination. As has been previously mentioned, this was allegedly done with Pope John Paul I, who only lasted 33 days, and John Paul II, who was more fortunate. The Jesuits are no respecters of persons and their political intrigue certainly extends into the Vatican, as it always has. While their task is to subjugate everyone to the Pope/Antichrist, they care not who that individual may be, as they ultimately serve Satan. The Jesuits will do anything to destroy the life or reputation of anyone who dares to stand in their way. They have been thrown out of fifty different countries, including seven times from England and nine times from France.[1] The U.S. has never yet expelled them due to their success in controlling politics, U.S. immigration, the economy, and especially the media. A prime example would be the constant harassment of duly elected president Donald J. Trump. The political coup to try to remove him from office has likely been the work of the Jesuits through their agents in our congress and media. It is more than interesting that I found a picture on Google images of Speaker of the House Nancy Pelosi kneeling before the Pope and kissing his ring. Is misplaced loyalty the reason for her shameful behavior? President Trump has stood solidly for our constitutional republic and against the deep state, swamp, establishment, which are many terms used to describe those traitors in our country pushing for a globalist New World Order.

Most of the books that expose the bloody history of the Jesuits are either missing, destroyed, or out of print. Fortunately, God raised up a high-ranking Jesuit, Dr. Alberto Rivera, who was converted to Christ, and provided much insider information about the Jesuits which would have otherwise been impossible. His wife suspects his death was the result of poisoning, but fortunately he first was able to share his story and a wealth of information with Chick Publications (chick.com). They printed a series of magazines called the Alberto series which documents his information and validity. The Catholic Church screamed phony and went to work to destroy any records proving his credibility. Fortunately, prior to this cover-up, Dr. Rivera provided indisputable documentation to Chick Publications.

A few examples of Jesuit intrigue follow to illustrate how they operate:

The Gunpowder Plot of 1605 was the name given to a conspiracy for blowing up King James I (of King James Bible fame) and the British Parliament on the 5th of November 1605. Complicit in this conspiracy was Henry Garnett, Superior of the English Jesuits, though it was carried out by the following devoted Catholics: Guy Fawkes, Robert and Thomas Wintour, Thomas Percy, Christopher and John Wright, Francis Tresham, Everard Digby, Ambrose Rookwood, Tho-mas Bates, Robert Keyes, Hugh Owen, John Grant and the man who is said to have organized the whole plot, Robert Catesby. The Jesuits rarely do the dirty work, but usually recruit others to carry out their plans. In this case, thirty-six barrels of gunpowder were concealed in a room underneath the House of Lords where King James I was scheduled to meet with Parliament on November 5, 1605. The plot was uncovered when Lord

Monteagle received a letter from his conspirator cousin, Francis Tresham, warning him not to attend Parliament that day. Guards were dispatched and discovered Guy Fawkes, the explosive expert who was to set off the explosion. He was then interrogated with torture to gain the names of his co-conspirators, who were apprehended and executed.

Many other examples can be given of Jesuit intrigue throughout Europe, of which the French Revolution is most notorious. But let's jump ahead to a prime example in the United States during our own civil war. The Jesuits played a huge role in fomenting our civil war. Charles Chiniquy was a faithful Roman Catholic priest who later converted to Christ and wrote the book, Fifty Years in the Church of Rome. He was a contemporary of Abraham Lincoln and became his close friend. In this book he exposes the plan to overthrow the United States and also documents how the Jesuits were responsible for the assassination of Abraham Lincoln. The Jesuit plan was to flood our shores with Catholic immigrants from Europe to move into our big cities and gain political power in both voting blocks, and also to promote faithful Roman Catholics into positions of influence as teachers, policemen, judges, senators, and congressmen.

In 1852 Chiniquy attended a conference in Buffalo, New York at the invitation of D'Arcy McGee. Mr. McGee was editor of The Freeman's Journal, the official journal of the Bishop of New York. The following was said at that conference composed principally of priests:

"We are also determined to take possession of the United States; but we must proceed with the utmost secrecy and wisdom. Silently and patiently, we must mass our Roman Catholics in the great cities of the United States, remembering that the vote of a poor journeyman, though he be covered with rags, has as much weight in the scale of power as the millionaire Astor, and that if we have two votes against his one, he will become as powerless as an oyster. Let us pray God that they continue to sleep a few years longer, waking only to find their votes outnumbered as we will turn them forever, out of every position of honor, power and profit! When not a single judge or policeman, will be elected if he be not a devoted Irish Catholic! What will those so-called giants think when not a single senator or member of Congress will be chosen, unless he has submitted to our holy father the pope! We will not only elect the president, but fill and command the armies, man the navies and hold the keys of the public treasury. ... then we will rule the United States, and lay them at the feet of the Vicar of Jesus Christ, that he may put an end to their godless system of education, (at that time Christian/ protestant), and the impious laws of liberty of conscience which are an insult to God and man!"[2]

In current days the flood of immigrants comes mainly from the strongly Catholic countries south of our border. Does it now make sense why we are currently having such problems with immigration and why our government institutions and leaders consistently act contrary to the dictates of our constitution and our true Christian heritage?

Mr. Chiniquy stated that as a priest, "My professors of philosophy, history, and theology had been unanimous in telling me that the principles and laws of the Church of Rome were absolutely antagonistic to the laws and principles which are the foundation stones of the Constitution of the United States".[3] Chiniquy later faced false charges by the local corrupt Catholic bishop he served under, in collaboration with several corrupt priests. Chiniquy was targeted as a priest for revering the Bible above the Pope and fighting the liquor traffic, among other conflicts. He was successfully defended by an attorney known as honest Abe. Abraham Lincoln, in winning the case, exposed the corruption of the bishop and priests and was put on Rome's

203

hit list. He also interfered with the major coup the Vatican had planned for the United States, which we know as the Civil War.

When the Jesuits had the right number of Catholics in place, through immigration, they used one of their favorite techniques of divide and conquer. The issue of slavery was the perfect vehicle and through the controlled media, they fanned the flames of passion on both sides. During the ensuing presidential race, they made an enormous promotion of their pawn, Democratic Senate leader, Stephen A. Douglas, who said, "I don't believe the Negro is any kin of mine at all." Republican Abraham Lincoln was viciously slammed in the Jesuit controlled newspapers nationwide, being called an ape, stupid brute, most dangerous lunatic, a bloody monster, etc. In God's providence he still won the presidency on November 6, 1860, to the dismay of the Catholic hierarchy. One month after Lincoln's election, South Carolina pulled out of the United States. Ten other states seceded in short order and elected Jefferson Davis as the new President of the Confederate States of America. Davis ordered General PGT Beauregard to attack Fort Sumter and the bloodbath began in our beloved country. The only foreign power to endorse and support the Confederate States of America and acknowledge Jefferson Davis as its President was the Vatican. As Lincoln traveled to Washington, D.C. for his inauguration, Catholic hit men were waiting in Baltimore, Maryland to assassinate him. His secret service found out and transferred him to a midnight train, which arrived safely.

During a meeting between priest Charles Chiniquy and Abraham Lincoln sometime after his inauguration, Lincoln stated to Chiniquy, "I am so glad to meet you again," he said: "you see that your friends, the Jesuits, have not yet killed me. But they would have surely done it when I passed through their most devoted city, Baltimore, had I not passed by incognito a few hours before they expected me. We have proof that the company which had been selected and organized to murder me was led by a rabid Roman Catholic, called Byrne; it was almost entirely composed of Roman Catholics; more than that, there were two disguised priests among them, to lead and encourage them. I am sorry to have so little time to see you: but I will not let you go before telling you that, a few days ago, I saw Mr. Morse, the learned inventor of electric telegraphy: he told me that when he was in Rome, not long ago, he found out the proofs of a most formidable conspiracy against this country and all its institutions. It is evident that it is to the intrigues and emissaries of the Pope that we owe, in great part, the horrible civil war which is threatening to cover the country with blood and ruins. I am sorry that Professor Morse had to leave Rome before he could know more about the secret plans of the Jesuits against the liberties and the very existence of this country."[4]

Throughout his presidency Lincoln consistently was betrayed and disobeyed by pro catholic generals and members of his cabinet. Please understand that there were good and godly men on both sides of the conflict fighting for what they believed were just causes. Unfortunately, as in many wars, they were pawns of a grand design for world domination by the Vatican. On April 14, 1865, just five days after the Civil War had ended, Abraham Lincoln went to Ford's theatre with his wife, Mary Todd Lincoln on Good Friday. She recalled his last words as they sat there: He said he wanted to visit the Holy Land and see those places hallowed by the footprints of the Savior. He was saying there was no city he so much desired to see as Jerusalem. And with the words half spoken on his tongue, the bullet of the assassin entered the brain, and the soul of the great and good President was carried by the angels to the New Jerusalem above.[5]

Dr. Alberto Rivera, ex-high ranking Jesuit priest under the Extreme Oath of Induction, was told the following information by Jesuit historians: That after Lincoln's assassination the Vatican ordered Catholic writers to immediately write Lincoln's biography and destroy his reputation, and Christian testimony. Protestant authors influenced by the Vatican made the same attack. Some of their claims were that Lincoln was supposed to be agnostic, a mason, into séances, a free thinker, an atheist, etc.[6] Let's allow Lincoln to speak for himself concerning his faith in Christ: In 1865, not long before he was assassinated, a clergyman from Illinois asked Lincoln, "Do you love Jesus?" President Abraham Lincoln told him how being at Gettysburg had affected him in that regard:

"When I left Springfield, I asked the people to pray for me. I was not a Christian. When I buried my son, the severest trial of my life, I was not a Christian. But when I went to Gettysburg and saw the graves of thousands of our soldiers, I then and there consecrated myself to Christ. I do love Jesus."[7]

Charles Chiniquy states in his book, "After 20 years of constant and most difficult researches, I come fearlessly today before the American people to say and prove that the President, Abraham Lincoln was assassinated by the Jesuits of Rome."[8] During the trial of the conspirators, the Roman Catholic issue was a powder keg. Evidence of a Catholic conspiracy would have re-ignited another civil war. Eight conspirators were found guilty, with four being hung and four receiving prison sentences. The Jesuits instructed three of these to conceal their Catholic faith and be attended by Protestant ministers for public relations sake. Those hung were Mary Surratt, known as one of the most devout Catholic women in Washington, D.C.; Lewis Payne, who stabbed Secretary of State Seward; Dewey Herold, who was to assassinate Vice President Johnson; and George Atzerodt, who helped Booth escape the theater. John Wilkes Booth, who was the one who actually shot Lincoln was killed in a shoot-out on April 26. Around his neck was a medal of the Virgin Mary. All of the conspirators felt as though they were martyrs for God, much as do the Muslim suicide bombers. John Wilkes Booth said in his diary, "I can never repent: God made me the instrument of his (Lincoln's) punishment." All of these conspirators met in the home of Mary Surratt with Jesuit priests, who were there day and night prior to the assassination. Mary Surratt, the day after the assassination said in the company of several witnesses, "The death of Abraham

Lincoln is no more than the death of any nigger in the army." This was consistent with the decision of devout Roman Catholic Judge Taney in the Dred Scott case, in which he pronounced, "the Negroes have no right which the white is bound to respect."[9] General Baker, a learned and great patriot, in his report on the conspiracy, noted that "every conspirator in custody is by education a Catholic".[10]

Evidently, these conspirators never read the Bible, which says, *Thou shalt not kill* (Exodus 20:13); and *But I say unto you, Love your enemies, bless them that curse you, do good to them that hate you, and pray for them which despitefully use you, and persecute you* (Matthew 5:44); and two written specifically to the Church at Rome: *Let every soul be subject unto the higher powers (government). For there is no power but of God: the powers that be are ordained of God* (Romans 13:1); and *Dearly beloved, avenge not yourselves, but rather give place unto wrath: for it is written, Vengeance is mine; I will repay, saith the Lord* (Romans 12:19).

As this information may seem far-fetched to some, especially devout Catholics, let me give further proof of its veracity. Thomas M. Harris was a Brigadier General on the military commission that tried and condemned the conspirators. He was privy to all the information regarding Lincoln's assassination. He later presented this information in detailed documentation in the book, Rome's Responsibility for the Assassination of Abraham Lincoln. In this book, he gives carefully documented evidence of the activities of the conspirators and their connections to the Jesuits and the Vatican. He often cites their daily activities and often hour by hour details leading up to the assassination. His conclusion is as follows: "That the execution of this conspiracy in Lincoln's case, was delegated by the Pope of Rome to the Jesuits aided and abetted by the priests of Canada and Washington, D.C. in the United States and their lay agents, the Leopoldines."[11] (The Leopoldines were formed in Vienna in 1828, and called the Saint Leopold Foundation. It is a vast spy network through which the Jesuits operate.)

As further proof, a law was passed in Congress in 1867, in response to Lincoln's assassination, forbidding diplomatic relations with the Vatican. This law was repealed quietly during the Reagan administration, and Pio Laghi, the Vatican prelate was given access to U.S. government vehicles and privileges, to promote the Roman Catholic Church in America. How revealing that many Jesuit front groups like the A.C.L.U., Americans United for Separation of Church and State, and others, never spoke one word in protest to this obvious violation of the first amendment.

Similar to the presidency of Lincoln, we are seeing an amazingly similar scenario playing out in the presidency of Donald J. Trump. For those who don't believe the lies and half-truths of the liberal press, we see another attempted political coup, taking place to destroy our country.

Let's look back at WWII. In Italy, a brutal leader named Benito Mussolini was swept into power by the Catholic vote directed by the Vatican. The Black Pope assigned a top Jesuit named father Tacchi Venturi as his priest confidant and father confessor. Pope Pius XI called Mussolini "The man whom providence allowed us to meet." Mussolini signed a concordat with the Vatican, and re-established the Pope's temporal power giving the clergy complete power over Italy. Meanwhile Germany was in shambles. There was an attempt to refashion Germany into a republic, but this was effectively stopped by the Jesuits through the efforts of two men, Franz Von Papan and Cardinal Pacelli, who later became Pope Pius XII. The Jesuit father Staempfle wrote a book, Mein Kampf, for a man named Adolf Hitler. It was their master plan to take over Germany, and Hitler, trained by the Jesuits in his youth, was their man. He was an artist with a gift for fiery and moving oration that was noticed and exploited. Hitler's brown shirts, the predecessors of the Gestapo, clubbed and beat all opposition into submission, including Roman Catholics. The Jesuits built the Third Reich as their second front after Italy. They chose as their symbol an old occult emblem, the Swastika.[12] Von Papen boasted that "The Third Reich is the first power, which not only recognizes, but puts into practice, the high principles of the Papacy."[13] The third front was Franco of Spain. All three of these governments had concordats with the Vatican and were working on its behalf. The German secret service, known as the Gestapo, was headed by Heinrich Himmler, and organized by the Jesuits. Himmler's uncle was a Jesuit who was one of his superior officers. What we know as the Holocaust, was in essence a Roman Catholic inquisition with the number of victims several times larger than six million, when Christians and others are included. After Hitler lost, the Jesuits carefully covered their tracks to any association between Hitler and the Vatican. However, the Spanish National Newspaper declared, "Adolf Hitler, son of the Catholic Church, died while defending Christianity." For more detail on Jesuit/Vatican involvement in WWII, I would strongly recommend The Godfathers-Alberto part 3, published by Chick Publications, Chino, Ca. 91706. The United States entering the war thwarted the plans of the Vatican as Hitler and the Nazi powers went down to defeat.

At that point in time the Men in Black had not gained sufficient influence in the United States, but that progressively changed. The United States has been the biggest thorn in the flesh to the Vatican and their major target. In 1960, John F. Kennedy became the first Roman Catholic President. During his tenure the Supreme Court effectively removed prayer and the Bible from our public schools in 1962 and 1963. In 1963 President Kennedy was tragically assassinated. After that time the lines between Catholics and Christians became increasingly blurred.

Twenty years later a charming movie actor who was portrayed as a conservative man of faith was elected President. According to Dr. Alberto Rivera, there was a sign given to Jesuits who were under the Extreme Oath worldwide, indicating when the Ecumenical Movement had successfully wiped-out Protestantism in America, in preparation for the signing of a concordat with the Vatican. The sign was that a president would take the oath of office facing an Obelisk, the Washington Monument.[14] The Obelisk is an ancient pagan phallic (sexual) symbol prominent in Egypt, but also located in the Vatican and in our nation's capital. It's four sides represent the four corners of the earth, with a pyramid at the top. It represents one world government (NWO) and sexual reproduction. On January 20, 1981, for the first time in American history, the swearing in ceremony was moved from the east side of the White House to the west side facing the Washington Monument. President Ronald Wilson Reagan was the first to be inaugurated facing an Obelisk.[15]

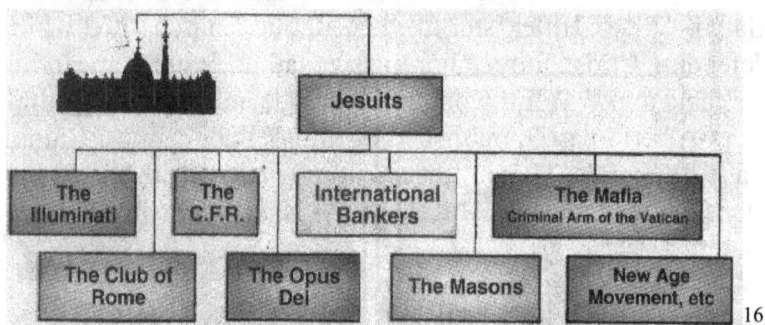

16

This is a very simple chart which shows a few of the main front organizations of the Jesuits. It is literally the tip of the iceberg. Hollywood and the entertainment industry would be positioned underneath the Mafia. The Tri Lateral Commission and Bilderbergers would be under the CFR and Witchcraft and Politics would fall under the Illuminati. Many times, the interconnections and relationships are closely aligned and the lines are blurred. This would especially be true of the Mafia and the Illuminati. The press or news media could fall under both the Illuminati and the Council on Foreign Relations (CFR). The environmental (green) movement and ecumenical movements would fall in the block with the New Age movement. While these groups are often at odds with each other, the overseeing control is the Jesuit order with their goal of a one world church (Pope/False Prophet) and one world ruler (Pope). Let me mention again that many underlings in these groups and subgroups are ignorant pawns who think they are serving just causes.

When a common Jesuit is elevated to a position of command or special assignment, he takes a special oath which binds his soul. It is called the Extreme Oath of Induction. The following excerpt will reveal the true nature and intentions of the Black Knights:

"I furthermore promise and declare that I will, when opportunity present, make and wage relentless war, secretly or openly, against all heretics, Protestants and Liberals, as I am directed to do, to extirpate and exterminate them from the face of the whole earth; and that I will spare neither age, sex or condition; and that I will hang, waste, boil, flay, strangle and bury alive these infamous heretics, rip up the stomachs and wombs of their women and crush their infants' heads against the walls, in order to annihilate forever their execrable race. That when the same cannot be done openly, I will secretly use the poisoned cup, the strangulating cord, the steel of the poniard or the leaden bullet, regardless of the honor, rank, dignity, or authority of the person or persons, whatever may be their condition in life, either public or private, as I at any time may be directed so to do by any agent of the Pope or Superior of the Brotherhood of the Holy Faith, of the Society of Jesus."

This oath is taken from the book Subterranean Rome by Carlos Didier, translated from the French and published in New York in 1843. Dr. Alberto Rivera escaped from the Jesuit Order in 1967, and he describes his Jesuit oath in exactly the same way as it appears in this book. Semper idem: always the same. The Jesuit Oath of Induction was also recorded in the Congressional Record of the U.S.A. (House Bill 1523,

Contested election case of Eugene C. Bonniwell, against Thos. S. Butler, Feb. 15, 1913, pp. 3215-3216). It was removed in recent years in violation of U.S. Law, but many people still have the documentation on it.

It is obvious that they are very serious about their mission. Like the Masons, the Jesuits at the lower levels have little idea what the people at the top truly believe and what their goals are. This is why secrecy is so important to them and why Jesus and the Bible forbid secret oaths.

But I say unto you, Swear not at all; neither by heaven; for it is God's throne: Nor by the earth; for it is his footstool: neither by Jerusalem; for it is the city of the great King (Matthew 5:34,35).
But above all things, my brethren, swear not, neither by heaven, neither by the earth, neither by any other oath: but let your yea be yea; and your nay, nay; lest ye fall into condemnation (James 5:12).

Is it possible to serve Satan under the name of Jesus? Jesus himself warned three times in Matthew 24:5; Mark 13:6; and Luke 21:8, *For many shall come in my name, saying, I am Christ; and shall deceive many.* Satan is great in deceiving people by complicating things so that men will trust in his false prophets. He makes things deep and dark and mysterious. Jesus is the opposite. Though infinite in intelligence as Almighty God, he makes his message so simple that a child can understand it. He always spoke in simple language when communicating his great truths in contrast to the priests who wowed people with their rituals and traditions. Jesus said in Mark 7:13, *Making the word of God of none effect through your tradition, which ye have delivered: and many such like things do ye.* Later the Apostle Paul warned in Colossians 2:8, *Beware lest any man spoil you through philosophy and vain deceit, after the tradition of men, after the rudiments of the world, and not after Christ.*

My dear friend, if you are still having trouble believing the evidence in this book, let me suggest that you have been conditioned from an early age to look at Jesus Christ and the Bible through the eyes of men rather than looking at men through the eyes of Jesus Christ and His Word, the Bible. If you have not yet put your faith and trust in Jesus Christ alone, I urge you to do it before it is too late. In our last section I will explain the Jesuit plan for the taking over America and God's plan for your life and eternity.

Chapter 21

Rome's Mysterious Movements and God's Miraculous Message

S ome things at this point should be apparent concerning the 'Unholy Trinity'.

First, there is a spiritual battle going on between God and the Devil.

Second, since the Devil cannot do anything to God, his focus is to destroy those who God desires as his children, namely mankind.

Third, the increasing numbers of catastrophic events such as floods, hurricanes, tornadoes, wildfires, earthquakes, pandemics, political turmoil, etc., are just a preview of what is to come. I believe they are Satan's effort to destroy mankind, and allowed by God as warning signs of the coming judgement. Jesus said they were the *beginning of sorrows*.

Fourth, Satan's greatest weapon is deception (indoctrination, fake news, propaganda, false doctrine), as the means of keeping people from the truth. Surprisingly, he uses religion as the most effective means of achieving this objective. Unfortunately, many cooperate with Satan knowingly, and many more unknowingly.

And **fifth**, the conspiracy of the Unholy Trinity, while most often referred to as the New World Order, or by conservative politicians as the deep state or the swamp, is headquartered in Rome, and more specifically, the Vatican. In the United States, our public school and university education system is indoctrinating students toward a global socialist society in collusion with our controlled news and entertainment media who most often proclaim the opposite of the truth. Is it possible that these together have enabled corrupt politicians to engage in a political coup to remove President Trump from his duly elected office, because he stood against the establishment and their goals? For the first time in American history the 2020 election accepted widespread mail in voting (different from absentee ballots), using the Covid 19 pandemic as a basis to change our constitutional safeguards, and enable possible widespread voter fraud. I believe this is all part of the plan to arrive at a one world socialist government and one world church.

While there are several religious movements today, we will focus on the key movement working to unite all others. This mysterious movement of Rome originated in the Vatican under the direction of the False Prophet, the Jesuit General. The Jesuit General at that time was Jean-Baptiste Janssens. Under orders from him, Pope John XXIII inaugurated the Trojan horse Ecumenical Movement under Vatican Council II. Pope John XXIII reigned from 1958 to 1963 and was considered a good Pope. A good Pope is one who fully follows the commands of his Jesuit General. This obedience actually got Pope John XXIII on the fast track to sainthood in the Roman Catholic Church as he is now known as Blessed John. The Ecumenical Movement employed the old adage, if you can't beat them, join them. Instead of calling everyone else heretics and using the inquisition model, it began a conciliatory approach to all other religions. The Mass was changed from Latin to English and they stopped proclaiming that salvation is in the Roman Catholic Church alone. The emphasis became sincerity and many Christian phrases were adopted, such as being born-again and receiving Christ, though with much different meanings. Under the teachings of Vatican II, sincere Communists, Buddhists, Hindus, Moslems, atheists, etc., were all going to Heaven. Among the multiplicity of changes brought about by Vatican II was the teaching that Protestants were no longer heretics, but separated brethren. This approach was necessary due to the

216

prominence and promulgation of the Bible in the United States. In a nutshell, it is the fatherhood of God and the brotherhood of man. We are all innately good and have a spark of the divine so that we are all the children of God. This man-made idea is clearly an affront to God, who gave His own Son Jesus, and contradicts what He clearly states in the scriptures. *Neither is there salvation in any other: for there is none other name under heaven given among men, whereby we must be saved.* (Acts 4:12)

While the Ecumenical Movement has birthed many and various religious movements, it is the main apparatus to bring about a one world church. While the Ecumenical movement was aimed mainly at liberal protestant denominations, its offshoot, the charismatic movement was aimed at Pentecostal and Full Gospel churches. The aim was to seduce them into fellowshipping with Catholics counterfeiting the gifts of the Spirit, including tongues, healing, and miracles. Most of the religious movements abounding today can be traced back to the Ecumenical movement and the Vatican, all with the same ultimate goal.

The ulterior motive in contradicting God's simple plan of salvation is to bring all separated brethren into the fold of the Roman Catholic Church and to ultimately bow to the Pope/Antichrist. When they regain dominance as they had in the dark ages, the facade of tolerance will disappear and the ultimate inquisition will occur. The 666 Universal Product Code system will ensure that if you don't worship the Antichrist, you will be unable to buy or sell. It will also isolate and identify you as a cancer in this world that needs to be eliminated. Under the direction of the False Prophet, anyone who will not take the *mark* and worship the Antichrist will be executed, often through being beheaded (Rev. 20:4). The Roman Catholic Church is only the means to an end for the Unholy Trinity. She is the woman that rides the Beast in Revelation Chapter 17, as was explained in the chapter on the Scarlet Harlot. Revelation, chapter 18 describes how she will be destroyed in one hour, when she is no longer needed by the Beast.

And I heard another voice from heaven, saying, Come out of her, my people, that ye be not partakers of her sins, and that ye receive not of her plagues. For her sins have reached unto heaven, and God hath remembered her iniquities. Reward her even as she rewarded you, and double unto her double according to her works: in the cup which she hath filled fill to her double. How much she hath glorified herself, and lived deliciously, so much torment and sorrow give her: for she saith in her heart, I sit a queen, and am no widow, and shall see no sorrow. Therefore shall her plagues come in one day, death, and mourning, and famine; and she shall be utterly burned with fire: for strong is the Lord God who judgeth her. (Revelation 18:4-8) *And saying, Alas, alas, that great city, that was clothed in fine linen, and purple, and scarlet, and decked with gold, and precious stones, and pearls! For in one hour so great riches is come to nought. And every shipmaster, and all the company in ships, and sailors, and as many as trade by sea, stood afar off, And cried when they saw the smoke of her burning, saying, What city is like unto this great city!* (Revelation 18:16-18)

That will be a very bad day to be a priest, nun, or other official in the Roman Catholic Church. Because her complete destruction shall come in one hour, it seems likely that she will be hit with a nuclear bomb or missile. The world at large is headed for a nuclear holocaust that is unimaginable. How can people *come out of her*, so they are not *partakers of her sins, and receive not of her plagues*? And is there anything we can do to thwart the Unholy Trinity, either individually or corporately?

While it may appear that the outlook is bleak, and the odds against us are overwhelming, there is great news! Anyone plus

218

God is a majority! The Bible says, *What shall we then say to these things? If God be for us, who can be against us* (Romans 8:31)? The members of the Unholy Trinity are scared of the truth, and God has made the truth so simple and obvious that a five-year-old child can understand it. The truth is centered in what is called the Gospel, which literally means good news. It is summed up in two verses of the Bible:

> *For I delivered unto you first of all that which I also received, how that Christ died for our sins according to the scriptures; And that he was buried, and that he rose again the third day according to the scriptures.* (1Corinthians 15:3,4)

This is God's provision for our salvation, and it is the only way of salvation. Jesus himself declared, *I am the way, the truth, and the life: no man cometh unto the Father, but by me* (John 14:6). Some people foolishly argue that this is a very narrow view of going to heaven, despite heaven being billions of light years away. Most people are clueless about where it is, and yet they think there must be other ways to get there besides Jesus. These same people have no problem with the fact that misdialing one number in a phone number will not connect them to their party, or missing one character in an email address would do the same. They think that reaching a destination in the far reaches of space should be less precise and that man deserves to have a voice in how to get to God's Heaven.

Normally man complicates the way of salvation, but God made it simple. An event recorded in the Bible illustrates its simplicity. It is the experience of a prison guard in the town of Philippi, recorded in the book of Acts, chapter 16, verses 25-34. The Apostle Paul and Silas were in prison, having been falsely accused by the religious leaders. At midnight Paul and Silas were praying and singing, which was heard by both the prisoners and the guard. God sent an earthquake, opening the doors to the cells. The jailer thought prisoners had escaped and would have committed suicide rather than face torture and death for dereliction of duty by the Roman government. Paul and Silas intervened by calling to him and assuring him that all prisoners were secure. The jailer who had just faced eternity, came into their cell, fell on his knees, and asked them, *Sirs, what must I do to be saved* (Acts 16:30)? Their answer was simple and direct: *Believe on the Lord Jesus Christ, and thou shalt be saved, and thy house* (Acts 16:31). Notice that Paul and Silas did not point them to any church, religious leader, religious ritual or activity. They pointed him to Jesus Christ and his sacrificial death on the cross.

While this is easy to understand, some may wonder why Christ had to die on the cross. The simple answer is *for our sins*. As was mentioned earlier, sin is breaking God's law. His law is codified in what is known as the 10 Commandments. They are listed in the book of Exodus, Chapter 20, verses 1-17 and in the book of Deuteronomy, chapter 5, verses 6-21. I list them as follows:

1.   I am the LORD thy God... Thou shalt have no other gods before me.
2.   Thou shalt not make unto thee any graven image, or any likeness of any thing that is in heaven above, or that is in the earth beneath, or that is in the water under the earth: Thou shalt not bow down thyself to them, nor serve them: for I the LORD thy God am a jealous God, visiting the iniquity of the fathers upon the children unto the third and fourth generation of them that hate me; And shewing mercy unto thousands of them that love me, and keep my commandments.
3.   Thou shalt not take the name of the LORD thy God in vain; for the LORD will not hold him guiltless that taketh his name in vain.
4.   Remember the sabbath day, to keep it holy. Six days shalt thou labour, and do all thy work: But the seventh day is the sabbath of the LORD thy God: in it thou shalt

not do any work, thou, nor thy son, nor thy daughter, thy manservant, nor thy maidservant, nor thy cattle, nor thy stranger that is within thy gates: For in six days the LORD made heaven and earth, the sea, and all that in them is, and rested the seventh day: wherefore the LORD blessed the sabbath day, and hallowed it.
5. Honour thy father and thy mother: that thy days may be long upon the land which the LORD thy God giveth thee.
6. Thou shalt not kill.
7. Thou shalt not commit adultery.
8. Thou shalt not steal.
9. Thou shalt not bear false witness against thy neighbour.
10. Thou shalt not covet thy neighbour's house, thou shalt not covet thy neighbour's wife, nor his manservant, nor his maidservant, nor his ox, nor his ass, nor any thing that is thy neighbour's.

*If you check the 10 Commandments listed in the Bible against the 10 Commandments listed it the Catholic Church or their Catechisms, you will notice that the 2nd Commandment about making images is totally removed, though it is the most detailed. The 10th Commandment is split into the 9th and 10th. This is a serious matter since they erroneously say that obedience to the 10 Commandments is one of the requirements for entrance to Heaven. Sin is breaking God's commandments or anything that displeases God. God is HOLY. This means he is Sacred, Pure, and Perfect. The Bible says He cannot look upon sin. Even the smallest sin to him would be like a large spot of black grease on a pure white wedding dress. He says in James 2:10 *For whosoever shall keep the whole law, and yet offend in one point, he is guilty of all.* Years ago I was eating at a buffet and when I was ready to take my first spoonful of soup, I noticed a small cockroach in my bowl of soup. This was totally repulsive to me, and the cockroach, though small, ruined not only my bowl but the whole pot. Sin is so repulsive to God that he says if a man even looks upon a woman to lust, he is guilty of adultery. Whenever a law is broken, punishment must be meted out.

The main purpose, however, of God's 10 Commandments was to expose our sin and show us our need of the Savior, who took our punishment for us (Galatians 3:24,25). If we had no need of a Savior, God would certainly have never allowed His only begotten Son to suffer such a cruel death on the cross. While God reveals his plan of salvation throughout the Bible, God simplifies it especially in one book: Paul's epistle to the Church at Rome, known as the Book of Romans. There are just a few points for us to understand, as follows:

God says we are all sinners, *As it is written, There is none righteous, no, not one* (Romans 3:10). [no one is good enough to go to heaven], *For all have sinned, and come short of the glory of God* (Romans 3:23).

Imagine you and I were in a slam dunk contest with some of the greatest players in professional basketball. I wouldn't stand a chance. But suppose the hoop was set at 15 ft., just 5 ft higher, instead of the standard 10 ft. None of the NBA players could dunk either, though they may come closer or look better. Whether it would be a super athlete or the best dunker in professional basketball, no one can dunk on a hoop at 15 ft. above ground. An NBA star would miss the mark, just like a 90-year-old grandmother. We would all come short! We are used to man's standards, but God's is higher, much higher. He says in Isaiah 55:9, *For as the heavens are higher than the earth, so are my ways higher than your ways, and my thoughts than your thoughts.* We all come short of God's entrance requirements or standards, because we are sinners.

We are born sinners because of inheriting Adam's sin nature. *Wherefore, as by one man* (Adam) *sin entered into the world, and death by sin; and so death passed upon all men, for that all have sinned* (Romans 5:12). *For as by one man's disobedience many were made sinners, so by the obedience of one*

222

shall many be made righteous (Romans 5:19). We don't become sinners because we sin. We sin because we are sinners by nature. But that does not negate our accountability.

There is a serious penalty for sin. *For the wages of sin is death* (Romans 6:23a); *And death and hell were cast into the lake of fire. This is the second death. And whosoever was not found written in the book of life was cast into the lake of fire* (Revelation 20:14,15).

Jesus Christ warned repeatedly about Hell and the Lake of Fire. God proved that he wants no one to go there by providing a pardon at his own great expense.

God the Son, Jesus Christ, paid for all of our sins by his death on the cross. *But the gift of God is eternal life through Jesus Christ our Lord* (Romans 6:23b). *But God commendeth his love toward us, in that, while we were yet sinners, Christ died for us* (Romans 5:8).

He did not die for us because we loved and honored him, but while we were his enemies in rebellion against him. This death *was according to the scriptures*, in that he was crucified in precise fulfillment of Bible prophecy, and in that he *shed his blood*.

> *Forasmuch as ye know that ye were not redeemed with corruptible things, as silver and gold, from your vain conversation received by tradition from your fathers; But with the precious blood of Christ, as of a lamb without blemish and without spot:* (1Peter 1:18,19*) for it is the blood that maketh an atonement for the soul* (Leviticus 17:11b). God himself paid our penalty with His own blood!

We receive this gift of forgiveness and salvation by calling on Christ in repentance and faith. *For whosoever shall call upon the name of the Lord shall be saved* (Romans 10:13). Jesus said in Luke 13:3 and then again in verse 5, *I tell you, Nay: but, except ye repent, ye shall all likewise perish.*

Repentance is simply a change of mind and heart, admitting that God is right and we are wrong. It is not turning over a new leaf, or promising to, but rather a Godly sorrow resulting in a willingness to let Christ take the sin from our lives. Faith is simply believing what God says in the Bible. *For by grace* (God's unmerited favor) *are ye saved through faith; and that not of yourselves: it is the gift of God: Not of works, lest any man should boast* (Ephesians 2:8). To make it simple, repentance and faith are a matter of laying aside your indoctrination, opinions, and beliefs, and accepting what God clearly states in the Bible. It is trusting what God says about men, not what men say about God.

My dear friend, you may strongly disagree with some or much of what I have shared and may even be offended. That certainly was not my intent, but only to expose the truth regarding the Unholy Trinity and present you with God's simple plan of salvation. I can assure you that what I have shared is true. You may already be familiar with the simple plan of salvation and already have Christ as your Savior. If so, are you fighting the good fight of faith by being a witness for Jesus Christ? Would you help preserve our Constitutional freedoms by exposing the Unholy Trinity and using the Bible to influence our elected leaders?

On the other hand, maybe this is the first time you have heard God's plan of salvation and truth from the Bible and you are not one hundred percent certain where you will spend eternity. If you feel impressed with the simple truth I've shared, that is an indication that God's Holy Spirit is drawing you to himself as he did to me, many years ago. This is a great privilege not to be taken for granted or trifled with. *For he saith, I have heard thee in a time accepted, and in the day of salvation have I succoured* (come to aid or rescue) *thee: behold, now is the accepted time; behold, now is the day of salvation* (2 Corinthians 6:2). In Hebrews 3:7,8 God warns, *Wherefore as the Holy Ghost saith, Today if ye will hear his voice, Harden not your hearts, as in the provocation, in the day of temptation in the wilderness:*

When I reached the point in my life where I realized I was a sinner, under God's judgment, and that Jesus Christ died in my place, I knelt by my bedside and in a simple prayer acknowledged my sin and Christ's sacrifice for me, and asked him to save me. That simple act of believing and calling on him to save me resulted in me being *born again* into his family. While that sounds simple, anyone who knew me before and after would assure you that something supernatural happened to me.

If your desire is to call on Christ to save you, here is a simple model prayer you can pray:

Dear Lord Jesus, I admit that I have sinned against you. I believe in your sacrificial death, your burial, and resurrection to pay for my sins. I now choose to repent of my sin and call on you to be my Lord and Savior. I trust you alone and completely for my salvation. Amen.

While this is just a model, praying it with a sincere heart is sufficient for Christ to enter your life and change it forever. It will be authenticated by a new changed life; not sinless or perfect, but with new desires and a sensitivity to sin.

If you have received Christ as your Savior, let me urge you to follow the first step of obedience commanded by God through the Apostle Peter: Be baptized by immersion, Then Peter said unto them, *Repent, and be baptized every one of you in the name of Jesus Christ for the remission of sins, and ye shall receive the gift of the Holy Ghost* (Acts 2:38). Please note, baptism follows repentance and salvation. It does not precede it. The word baptism comes from the Greek word baptizo, pronounced bap-tid'-zo and means to immerse or submerge. Pray and ask the Holy Spirit to direct you to an independent, Bible believing church where the Bible is preached and people are invited to be saved. Tell the Pastor that you have trusted Christ as Savior and want to be scripturally baptized. This church should teach you the five simple keys to developing your relationship with Christ. They are:

- Faithful attendance in a Bible believing, preaching church.
- Faithfully reading/ studying the Bible.
- Communicating daily with God through prayer.
- Giving tithes and offerings to the church.
- Witnessing for Jesus Christ.

When these are practiced faithfully everything else should begin to fall into place.

My earnest desire in writing this book was to see people put their faith and trust in Jesus Christ and spend eternity in heaven. My secondary desire is to expose the awful Satanic trinity and their destructive plans. Would you please join with me in these two great missions?

If you have trusted Christ and would like some helpful literature or have questions, please email me at: knowthetruthmedia@gmail.com (include your name and address)

Bibliography

Part One, Chapter 4

1. The Humanist magazine, Jan./Feb. 1983, pg. 26
2. Harvard University. 1636. Stephen K. McDowell and Mark A. Beliles, America's Providential History (Charlottesville, VA: Providence Press, 1988), p. 91.
3. Harvard University. 1636. Quoted in Nancy Leigh De-Moss, ed., "How Christians Started the Ivy League," The Rebirth of America (Philadelphia, PA: Arthur S. DeMoss Foundation, 1986), p. 41. Peter Gay, A Loss of Mastery: Puritan Historians in Colonial America (Berkeley, CA: University of California Press, 1966), p. 23. Gary DeMar, America's Christian History: The Untold Story (Atlanta, GA: American Vision Publishers, Inc., 1993), p. 41.
4. Harvard University. 1636. "Our Christian Heritage," Letter from Plymouth Rock (Marlborough, NH: The Plymouth Rock Foundation), p. 2.
5. Private research conducted by Cullen Davis, P.O. Box 1224, Ft. Worth, TX 76101
6. Morris, Henry M. Scientific Creationism. EI Cajon, Calif.: Master Books, April 1985. (p. 169)
7. McLean, G. S.; McLean, Larry; Oakland, Roger. The Bible Key to Understanding the Early Earth. Oklahoma City, Okla.: Southwest Radio Church, 1987. (p. 26)
8. Huse, Scott M. The Collapse of Evolution. Grand Rapids, Mich.: Baker Book House, 1983. (p. 27)
9. Ackerman, Paul D. It's a Young World After All. Grand Rapids, Mich.: Baker Book House, 1986. (p. 26)
10. Huse, Scott M. The Collapse of Evolution. Grand Rapids, Mich.: Baker Book House, 1983. (p. 25)
11. Wysong, R. L. The Creation-Evolution Controversy. Midland, Mich.: Inquiry Press, 1976. (p. 177)
12. Huse, Scott M. The Collapse of Evolution. Grand Rapids, Mich.: Baker Book House, 1983. (p. 25)

13. Ibid. (p. 29)
14. Ackerman, Paul D. It's a Young World After All. Grand Rapids, Mich.: Baker Book House, 1986. (p. 45)
15. Blick, Edward F. A Scientific Analysis of Genesis. Oklahoma City, Okla.: Hearthstone Publ. Ltd., 1991. (p.26)
16. Morris, Henry M. Scientific Creationism. EI Cajon, Calif.: Master Books, April 1985. (p. 157)
17. Ibid. (p. 156)
18. Ibid. (p. 153)
19. Ibid. (p. 151)
20. McLean, G. S.; McLean, Larry; Oakland, Roger. The Bible Key to Understanding the Early Earth. Oklahoma City, Okla.: Southwest Radio Church, 1987. (p. 31)
21. Petersen, Dennis R. Unlocking the Mysteries of Creation. South Lake Tahoe, Calif.: Christian Equippers International, 1987. (p. 38)
22. Ibid. (p. 39)
23. McLean, G. S.; McLean, Larry; Oakland, Roger. The Bible Key to Understanding the Early Earth. Oklahoma City, Okla.: Southwest Radio Church, 1987. (p. 32)
24. Huse, Scott M. The Collapse of Evolution. Grand Rapids, Mich.: Baker Book House, 1983. (p. 23)
25. Ibid. (p. 25)
26. Morris, Henry M. Scientific Creationism. EI Cajon, Calif.: Master Books, April 1985. (p. 155)
27. Blick, Edward F. A Scientific Analysis of Genesis. Oklahoma City, Okla.: Hearthstone Publ. Ltd., 1991. (p.27)
28. Baker, Sylvia. Bone of Contention. Creation Science Foundation Ltd., Sunnybank, Queensland 4109 Australia: 1990. (p. 26)
29. Morris, Henry M. Scientific Creationism. EI Cajon, Calif.: Master Books, April 1985. (p. 167)
30. Petersen, Dennis R. Unlocking the Mysteries of Creation. South Lake Tahoe, Calif.: Christian Equippers International, 1987. (p. 39)
31. Ibid. (p. 40)

32. Morris, Henry M. Scientific Creationism. El Cajon, Calif.: Master Books, April 1985. (p. 160)
33. Hovind, Kent E. Creation Seminar, Parts 1-6 (most items
referenced onscreen-available from Creation Science
Evangelism, 29 Cummings Road, Pensacola, Fla. 32503).
34. Ibid.

Part One, Chapter 5

1. www.csun.edu/science/health/docs/tv&health.html Nor-
man Herr, Ph.D. California State University.

Part One, Chapter 6

1. Satanism in America, p.42

Part Two, Chapter 10

1. Mary Stewart Relfe, When Your Money Fails The "666"
System" is Here, 1981, pp. 56,57,58
2. Mary Stewart Relfe, The New Money System 666, 1982,
pp. xii, 206

Part Two, Chapter 12

1. The Rockefeller File, Gary Allen, 76 Press, pg. 182,183
2. David Rockefeller's Memoirs, Random House, New
York, 2002, pgs 404 and 405
3. The Rockefeller File, Gary Allen, 76 Press, pg. 31,32
4. Ibid., pg. 33
5. Ibid., pg. 33
6. Ibid., pg. 33
7. Ibid., pg. 34,35
8. USA Today, September 9, 1993.

Part Three, Chapter 15

1. The Pittsburgh Press, Saturday March 20, 1982, pg. B-12
2. https://discover.hubpages.com/religion-

philosophy/Virgin-Mary-Apparition-In-Clearwater-Florida

Part Three, Chapter 16

1. http://www.textweek.com/art/holy family.htm
2. Microsoft Encarta Encyclopedia, New Standard Encyclopedia., Vol. 9. pg. 0-155 & in 1936, Encyclopedia Britannica, Vol. 16, pg. 900-902

Part Three, Chapter 17

1. The Two Babylons, by Alexander Hislop; Babylon Mystery Religion, by Ralph Woodrow; Babylon Religion, by David W. Daniels; A Woman Rides the Beast, by Dave Hunt.
2. The Catholic Encyclopedia, Thomas Nelson 1976
3. McGee, J. Vernon, Thru the Bible with J. Vernon McGee, (Nashville: Thomas Nelson Publishers) 2000, c1981.

Part Three, Chapter 18

1. Halley's Bible Handbook, pg.774
2. Ibid.
3. Babylon Mystery Religion, Ralph Woodrow Evangelistic Association, pg. 93
4. Ibid., pg. 94
5. Ibid., pg. 94,95
6. www.tldm.org/news4/bernardin.htm (This is a Roman Catholic website.)
7. Ibid.
8. www.prose-n-poetry.com/display_work/10583 also, "In God's Name: An Investigation into the Murder of Pope John Paul I," (1984) Davis Yallop
9. Pope Leo XIII (from Encyclical Satis Cognitum: 9)
10. Modern Catholic Dictionary by John A. Hardon, S.J., copyright 1980
11. London Evening Standard, News & Current Affairs,

London, Monday 08.02.10 thisislondon.co.uk
12. Zenit 'The World Seen from Rome' www.zenit.org/article-18325?l=english ZE06113009 - 2006-11-30
13. "Spaniard becomes Jesuits' New 'Black Pope'". Reuters. 19 January 2008. Retrieved 29 November 2016.

Part Three, Chapter 19

1. The Spiritual Exercises of St. Ignatius of Loyola, Translated from the Autograph by Father Elder Mullen, S.J. New York: P.J. Kennedy and Sons, 1914.
This text is available in its entirety, along with many others from the Christian Classics Ethereal Library at Wheaton College.
2. The Force, Alberto Part Four, Vol. 15,, p. 24, Chick Publications, Inc.; Encyclopedia Britannia, I, Ignatius, 1911.
3. Will the New "Black Pope" Work? Time Magazine Saturday, Jan. 19, 2008
4. "The Jesuits", Malachi Martin, p. 94 Touchstone Books, Simon and Shuster, New York

Part Three, Chapter 20

1. The Jesuits, Chapter 27 www.Sundaylaw.net
2. Fifty Years in the Church of Rome, pgs. 281,282 Chick Publications 1985
3. Ibid., pg. 283
4. Ibid., pg. 292
5. Abraham Lincoln, the Christian, Johnstone, Abingdon Press, NY 1913, pg.182
6. The Big Betrayal, Chick Publications 1981, pg. 59
7. Words of Lincoln, Osborn H. Oldroyd, Mershon Company Press 1875, pg. 154
8. Fifty Years in the Church of Rome, Chick Publications 1985, pg. 309
9. Ibid., pg. 310
10. Ibid., pg. 311

11. Rome's Responsibility for the Assassination of Abraham Lincoln, Thomas M. Harris, Larry Harrison Publishing, St. John, IN 1999, pg. 260
12. Masonic and Occult Symbols Illustrated, Dr. Cathy Burns, Sharing 1998, pg. 332
13. The Godfathers, Chick Publications, 1982, Chino, Ca., pg. 20,21
14. Ibid., pg 26
15. Newsweek, Jan. 26, 1981, pg. 32
16. The Four Horsemen, Chick Publications, 1982, Chino, Ca, pg. 30

www.ingramcontent.com/pod-product-compliance
Lightning Source LLC
Chambersburg PA
CBHW060841280326
41934CB00007B/876